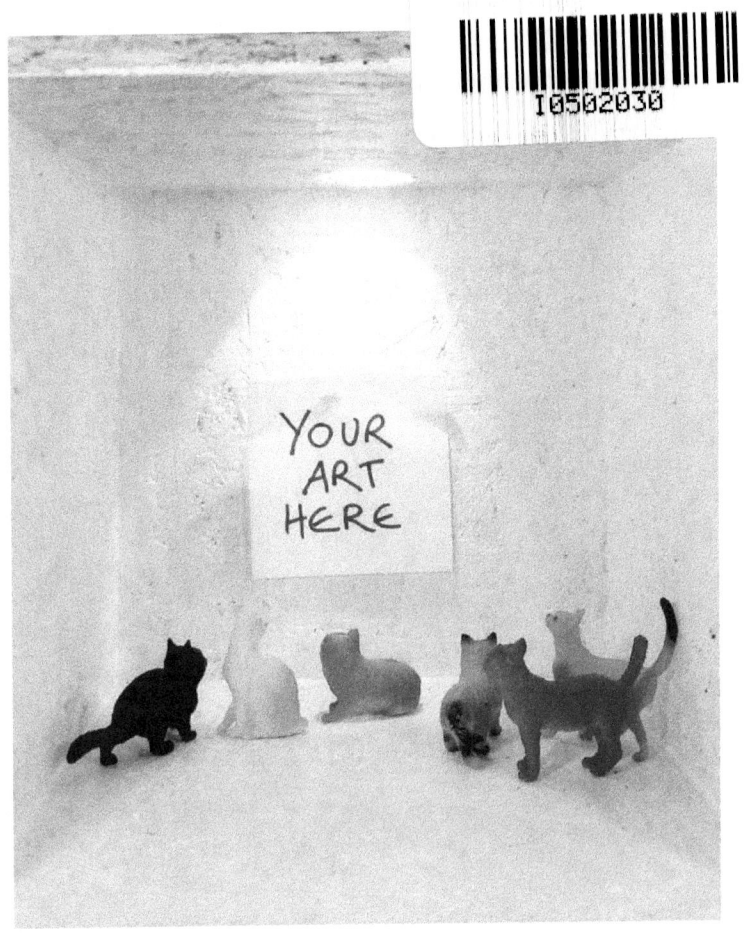

The Tiny Art Gallery Manual

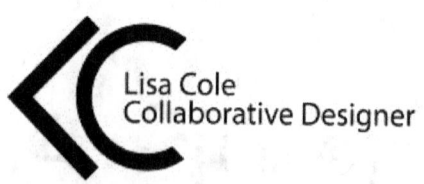

www.lisa-cole.co.uk

How to set up and promote your own tiny art gallery

By Lisa Cole from The Tiny Cat Gallery with contributions from

George Thom — Groock's Gallery
Jack Woodward — Cardboard Monkey Gallery
Lisa Fitzgerald — The Doll's House Art Gallery
Sally Eldars — The Open Dresser Gallery
Sam Toft — The Dog & Bone Gallery
Hondartza Fraga — Beyond Scale Gallery
Tiffany Struwig — Struwig Miniature Gallery
Indrė Ercmonaitė — Mini Gallery Don't Cry

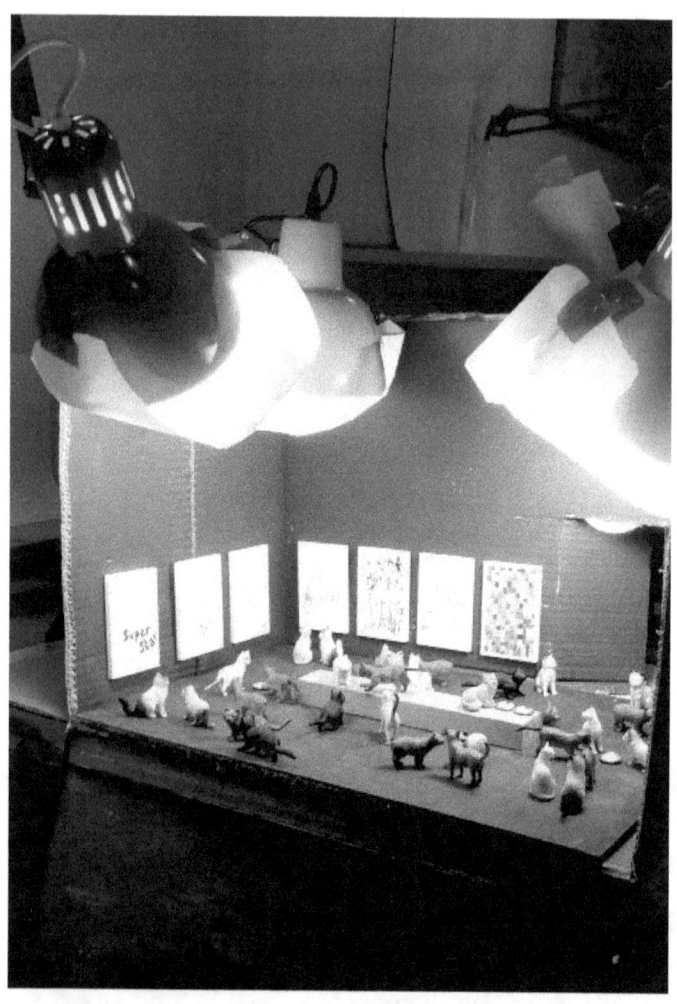

Behind the scenes at the Tiny Cat Gallery.
Private View of 'Retrospective' by Philip Ryland.

This cardboard box gallery is 50 cm wide and lit with anglepoise lamps covered in tissue paper to diffuse the light. The modern seating in the centre is a section of 2x1 inch timber.

A tiny gallery is any space that allows small artwork to appear large.

It can be meticulously detailed like a smaller replica of a real space, or it can be a basic cardboard box that represents the idea of a gallery.

A tiny gallery doesn't have to exhibit miniature art. A tiny gallery can be used to see what small artwork would look like if it was larger.

Contents

Background — 5
Tiny Galleries in History — 7
Why run a Tiny Gallery? — 9
Types of Tiny Gallery — 10
- Shelves and surfaces — 10
- Dolls houses — 11
- Virtual — 11

The Two Audiences — 15
- Human onlookers — 15
- Human participants — 15
- Travel like Gulliver — 17

Practicalities — 19
Gallery Requirements — 21
- Flooring — 21
- Walls — 22
- Displaying artwork — 23
- Lighting — 24
- Plinths — 25
- Seating — 25
- Doors and windows — 26
- Props — 27

Enforcing Scale — 29
Photography and Storytelling — 30
- Curator or critic? — 31

Types of events — 33

Curating — 35
Working with Artists — 36
- Have you agreed: — 36
- Artists details — 37
- Exhibition details — 37
- Artwork details — 39
- Artwork images — 39

Commerce — 43
Making Money — 44
Marketing on Social Media — 46
- Facebook — 46
- Instagram — 47
- Twitter — 48
- Pinterest — 48
- Gaining followers — 49
- Hashtags — 50
- Alternatives to social media — 51

Case Studies — 53
The Tiny Cat Gallery — 55
Groock's Gallery — 59
Cardboard Monkey Gallery (C.B.M) — 63
The Doll's House Art Gallery — 67
The Open Dresser (TOD) Gallery — 75
The Dog & Bone Gallery — 79
Beyond Scale — 85
Struwig Miniature Gallery — 91
Mini Gallery Don't Cry — 99

Resources — 103
Resources — 104
- Books and films — 104
- Admin — 106
- Scheduling — 107
- Graphic design — 108
- Hashtag ideas — 109
- Props and scaled figures — 110
- There is no right way — 111

Background

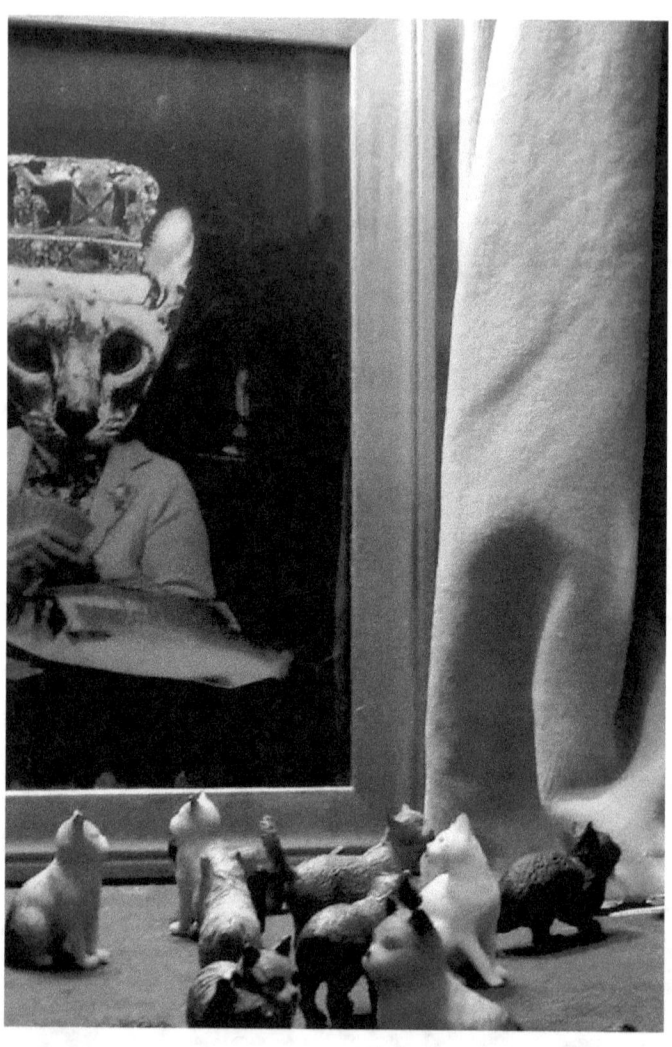

'A Feast to Remember'
Susan Plover at the Tiny Cat Gallery.

The artist wanted a grand environment for her digital collage so it was mounted in a gold frame with sumptuous velvet curtains surrounding it.

Tiny Galleries in History

From the 16th century, dolls houses with beautiful interiors were playthings for wealthy women to rival men's collections of curiosities. They were not devoted art galleries, but they were richly decorated and included paintings and sculptures. Designed for adults instead of children, this is the closest we get to a tiny gallery until the 20th century.

In 1934 Sydney Burney commissioned 34 famous modernist artists and sculptors to create work for a miniature gallery called the Thirty Four gallery. You can still see most of it today at Pallant House in Chichester. In tiny gallery terms it is pretty big, taking up an entire wall, but it is a good example of established artists taking small galleries seriously and exhibiting real, smaller than normal artwork.

This collection showed work from Barbara Hepworth, Ben Nicholson, Paul Nash, Henry Moore and Frances Hodgkins.

More recently, in 2019, The Thirty Four gallery inspired The 19 Gallery curated by Auckland Art Gallery. It included 19 small works by New Zealand artists who were inspired by Frances Hodgkins and her artwork at the Thirty Four Gallery.

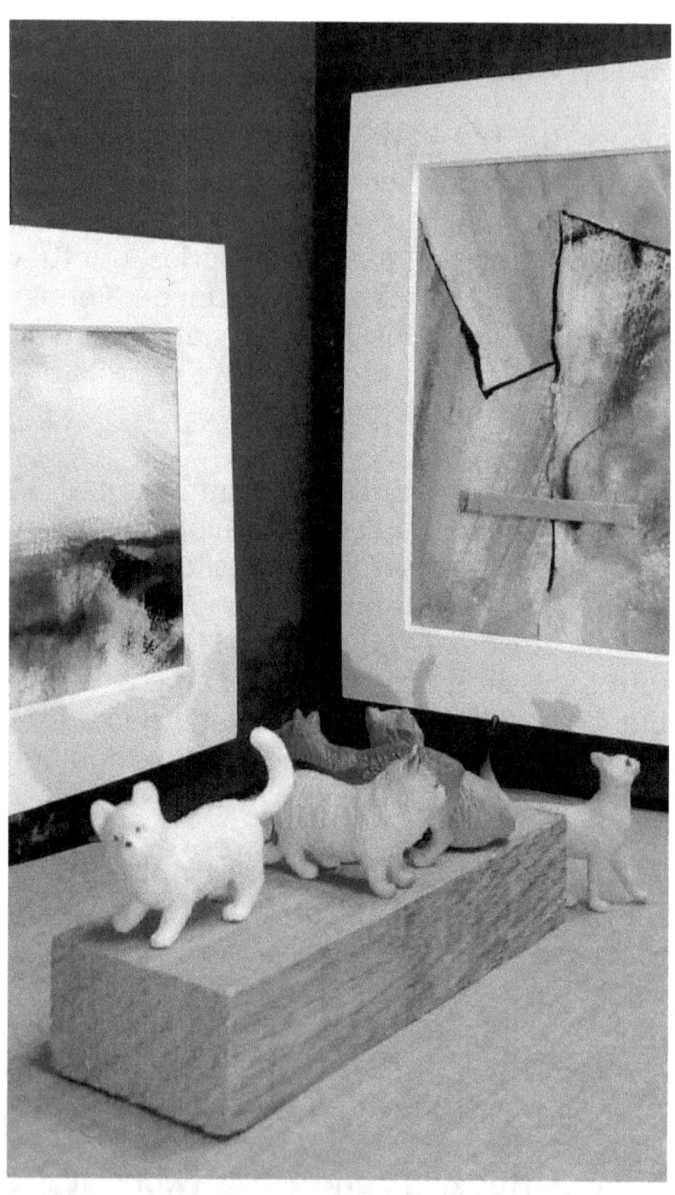

Sally Eldars' 'Seascapes' at the Tiny Cat Gallery.

Why run a Tiny Gallery?

It can be hard for very established artists to get into galleries. It sometimes feels impossible for new and emerging artists.

As an artist, running your own gallery will allow you to get an idea of how your work could look in a gallery setting. It will also give you a unique insight into what a gallery needs from creatives which will make working with them easier in the future.

If you are interested in curating exhibitions, a no risk step towards renting real space is to run a miniature version of a gallery. Your tiny gallery can be as simple or as detailed as you like as long as it gives a sense of artwork shown in a gallery space.

I recommend running a tiny gallery to anyone who creates or is interested in art. It will give you first hand experience of:

- Curating
- Display
- Lighting
- Photography
- Promotion
- Marketing

Types of Tiny Gallery

The bare minimum you need to start a tiny gallery is some artwork. As soon as you display it anywhere it creates it's own gallery.

There are no hard and fast rules; your gallery might be a sculpture garden or on a bookshelf.

Simply having a gallery mindset and seeing things from a different perspective is liberating.

You could start with a tour of your home to see what spaces work best as galleries.

Here are some basic ideas.

Shelves and surfaces

The top of a shelf will have a different spatial feeling in gallery terms to a middle shelf. Do you want your gallery to have traces of the original use in it?

Keeping books either side of artwork might be helpful to bring about a sense of size and scale.

Boxes

Wooden crates, shoe-boxes and biscuit tins all make excellent galleries. Unless you only want to view your gallery from above you will need to consider removing a wall or making a window for viewing and photography. You can turn a box on it's side to create a ready-made room.

Dolls houses

A ready made dolls house might seem like a quick solution for an instant tiny gallery but the tight space can be tricky to work with. However, the very housiness of a dolls house helps to create a sense of narrative. Stairs and doors bring scale and some dolls houses have built in lighting which can be an absolute gift.

Virtual

Your gallery does not have to exist in 3D at all. Virtual galleries don't have the usual restrictions of gravity which opens up a multitude of new curating possibilities.

The Tiny Gallery on Twitter (@thetinygallery) is a bot that shows different artworks in an ASCII gallery. It has lines to denote the gallery walls and often has images of very small people visiting.

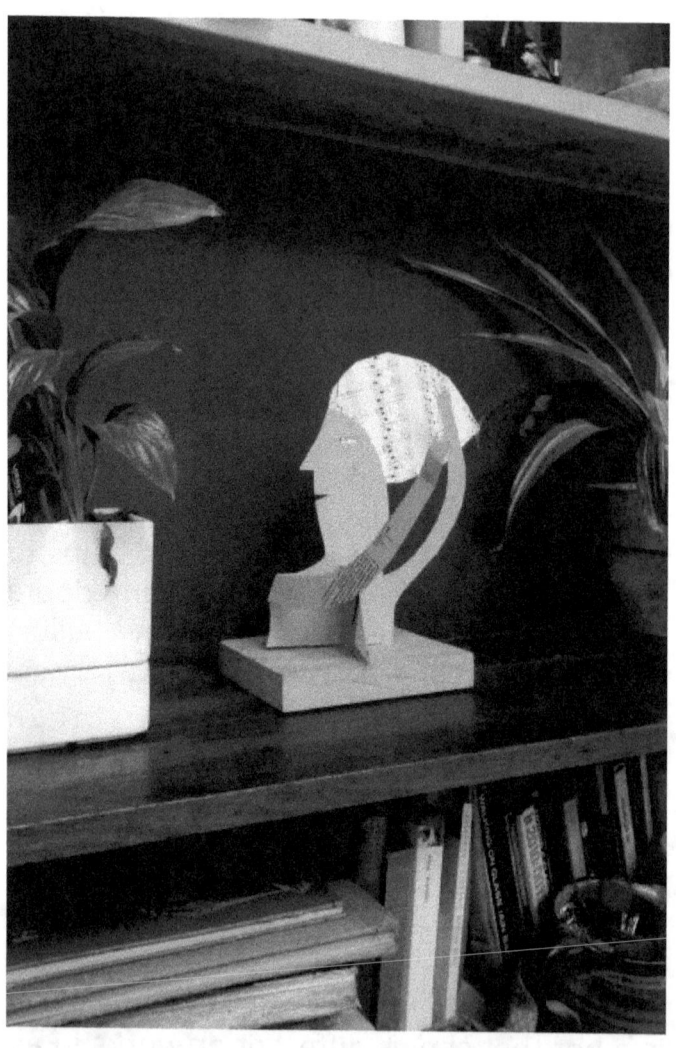

Lizzie Don's sculpture exhibited on a bookshelf.

Raised on a small wooden plinth, this sculpture stands out from the plants on a set of bookshelves. It is at waist height so the viewer looks down onto it.

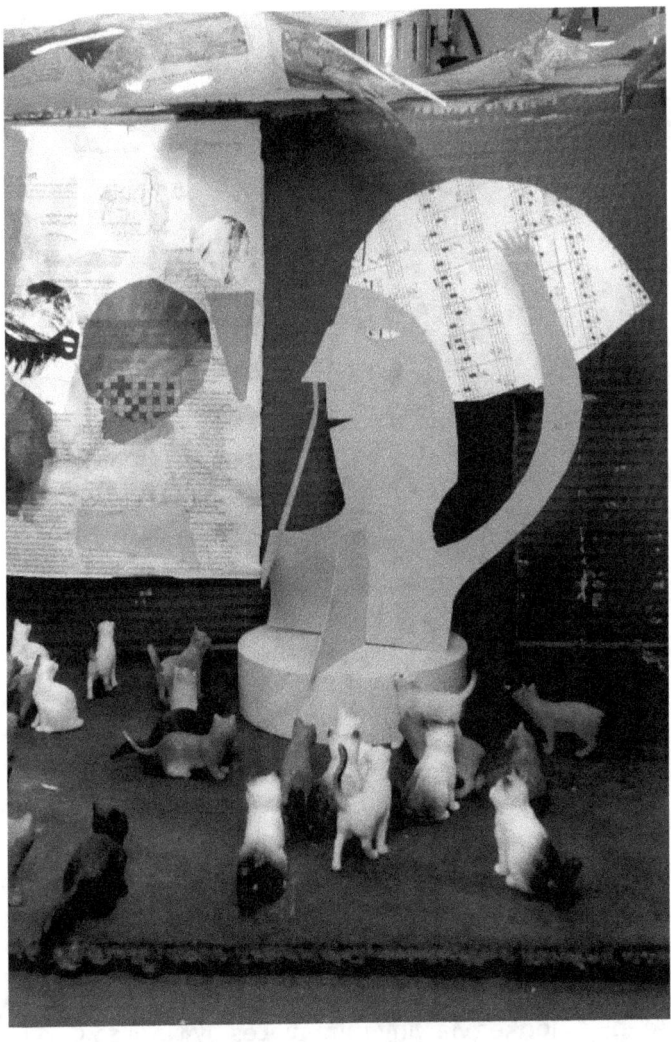

Lizzie Don's sculpture exhibited in a cardboard box.

The same sculpture set in a cardboard box gallery with small plastic cats to give a sense of scale has a very different feeling. It is so big; visitors have to look up to it as it dominates the space.

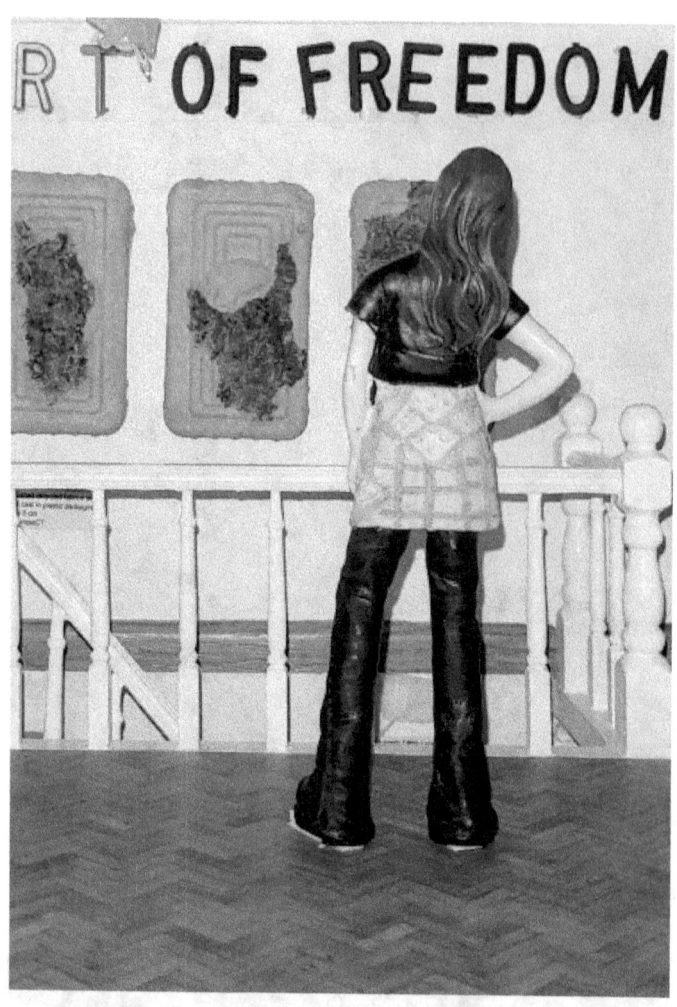

A tiny onlooker viewing mini-pieces by Nerissa Cargill Thompson at The Doll's House Art Gallery.

The detail really helps to scale the artwork. The intricate parquet floor and the turned balustrades on the staircase have a language that helps the viewer feel inside a home that has been renovated into a gallery.

The Two Audiences

With a small scale exhibition space you can have two main audiences:

- Full sized humans
- Scaled down figures

You can work with this in many ways. Do you want your human audience to think of your gallery as something small they can look at or as a tiny replica they can shrink down and visit? Is your human viewer an onlooker or a participant?

Human onlookers

If your human visitors are meant to perceive the exhibition as miniature they can peep into windows and through doorways. You might have an open roof or side view. The human is a voyeur looking in.

Human participants

If you show viewpoints from the scaled gallery visitors point of view, this will give the human viewers an idea of how the art would work at full scale. You will need to make the field of vision to be that of the scaled figures, either by photography or by limiting visual access.

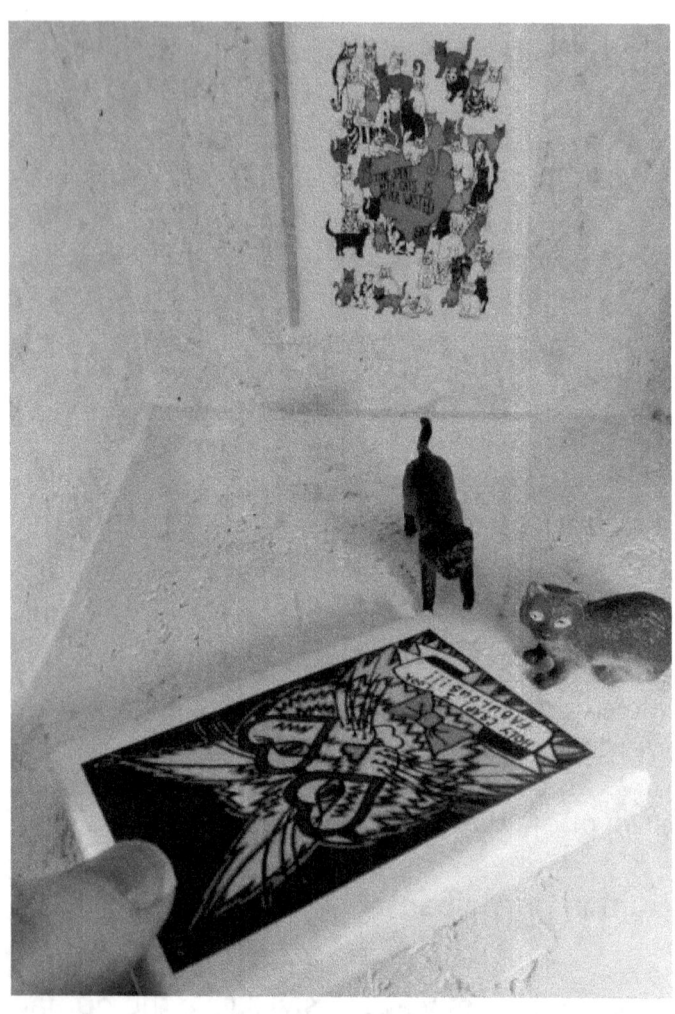

Small plastic cat technicians handing artwork over to a human at the Tiny Cat Gallery.

This photo was taken while packing down 'Catitude' by Victoria Shone. Shone mounted printed canvas onto tiny wooden stretchers to create depth.

Travel like Gulliver

You can always break fourth wall conventions and have your tiny figures interact with full sized humans through the invisible barrier that usually protects actors from the audience.

This strategy brings new narrative possibilities with the relationship between the humans and the scaled figures. Do they like each other? Who is the boss?

In the Tiny Cat Gallery the human is a mere servant. I've used the idea that cats are haughty and superior and translated it into the stories I tell via the gallery.

"**Don't start too small it can be a pain to downsize work and get the scale right.**"

Jack Woodward C.B.M. Galleries

Practicalities

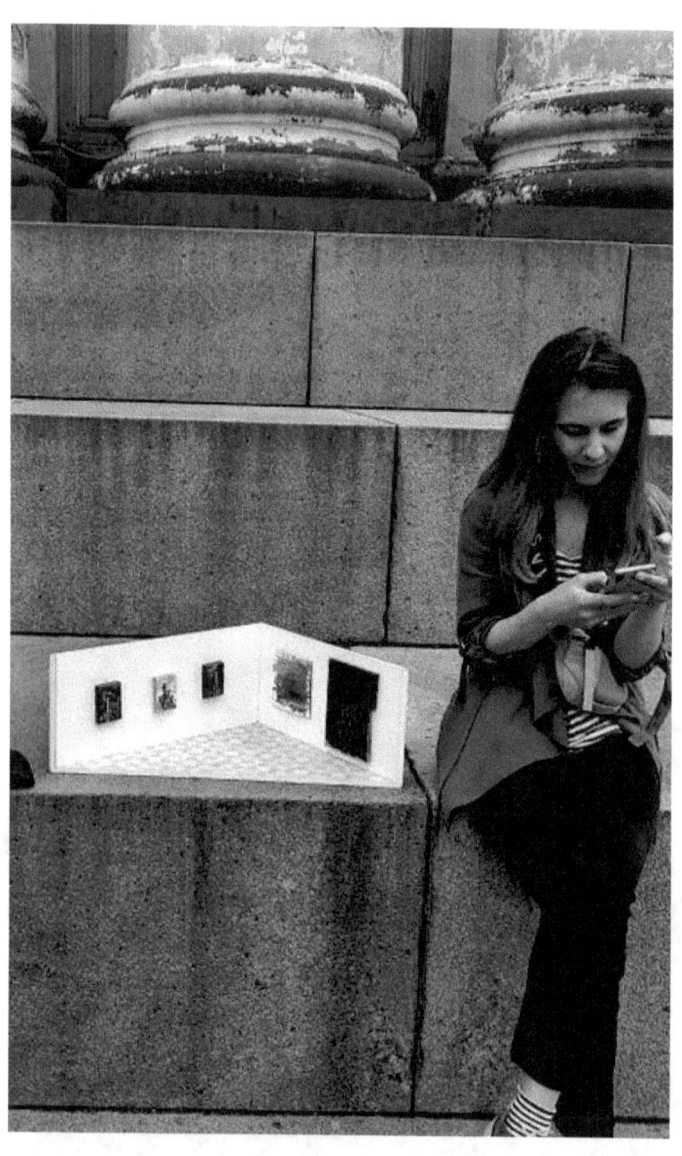

Akvilina Simkeviciute at Mini Gallery Don't Cry.

Gallery Requirements

If you are starting with an empty box this section will give you some ideas that will give viewers a rough sense of a gallery.

If you are interested in faithful or hyper realistic miniature galleries you might want to visit a dolls house or miniature railway supplier. A combination of both approaches would be very interesting.

Flooring

Changing floors can be a matter of cutting out a bit of paper if you run a tiny gallery.

You can get a look of concrete from cheap grey paper or the board that comes from the back of sketch books.

Carpet offcuts or samples are often given away by shops, (watch the pile length though as small scale figures can vanish in deep pile carpet.)

Old school sticky backed plastic or vinyl tiles can replicate marble well and a single plank of laminate flooring can make a stunning wooden floor.

Walls

What work will be displayed in your gallery? There are conventions to displaying art that you might want to follow. If you play by the rules it will be easier for your viewer to recognise a gallery setting but don't discount breaking away from tradition.

A gallery is typically plainly decorated to show the artwork off to its best. White cube galleries have been displaying modern art with minimal distraction since the 1920's. The background colour can be a frame for artwork, making it stand out, or recede.

Old masters are often displayed on darker backgrounds and at the National Gallery in London you can see deep and sumptuous coloured walls that work very well with gold framed oil paintings.

Unpainted is another option. Concrete gives an industrial feel. Timber walls can vary from rustic to polished mid century modern.

Think about the feel of your gallery. Is it cool and trendy or solid and reliable? If it was a full size space who would want to visit it?

Displaying artwork

If you are using figures to give a sense of scale you probably want to display the art at a height that suits them. Traditionally, the centre of the art is hung at eye-line level. For multiple works of different sizes use one as an anchor and work around it. Line them up so they are in a row at the bottom to make them easier on the eye or place them in clusters and groups both high and low if you want a more challenging exhibition.

Larger artworks can be hung facing slightly downwards instead of flat on the wall so they can be seen properly. Generally sticky tack works perfectly well to fix small artwork to most surfaces. If the art is heavy it might need some extra help and some artists prefer that it isn't used at all.

Pins work very well in cardboard walls. Stick a couple of pins halfway through the wall and rest stiff artworks on top. Remember the outside of the gallery will have sharp points which you can cover with sticky tack if you are worried about scratches. Pins can also be angled in to hold thinner work in place. There is no need to pierce the artwork, just use the pins to hold it.

If your walls are more solid try tiny pin tacks to hang work from but access might be an issue if you need to use a hammer.

Transparent nylon thread can be used to hang paintings or to suspend installations from the ceiling if you have one. If you don't have a ceiling use a ruler or wooden spoon across two walls to make a beam to hang from.

For lighter work and thinner walls try very strong magnets either side of the wall. Glue or tape the magnet to the back of the artwork and match it up with another magnet on the other side of the wall.

Lighting

What effect do you want from your lighting? Dark and moody or bright and open?

Whatever you want you are probably having to make do with lights from your home. Anglepoise lamps are great for tiny gallery lighting but try torches and reading lights as spotlights.

Rows of led lights can be found cheaply and can run from batteries, USB ports or the mains. You can cut them to length and use them under plinths or behind work too.

Harsh light produces strong shadows. Limit the shadows by diffusing the light. Tape tissue or thin paper over the lamp but keep clear of the bulb in case it is a fire risk. You can also bounce light around using sheets of white cardboard.

The trick is to think of how the light travels in straight lines from the bulb. If that light was a snooker ball, where would the edge of the table need to be to get it into the pocket? That is where your white cardboard needs to go if you want to reflect the light back on the subject.

In a darker space use the light to guide the viewers eyes to the artwork. A single down lit painting at the end of a dark gallery can be really effective.

Plinths

Plain white painted plinths are commonly seen in real galleries. These can be replicated by painting small boxes white or by using cubes of Styrofoam used in packaging.

For a more classic look the columns that separate wedding cakes make excellent plinths.

Seating

Seating brings an instant idea of scale to a tiny gallery. As soon as we see a chair we can imagine the size of person that would fit it and we apply that to any artwork nearby.

Plain chunks of wood make excellent modern bench seats and can be stacked up if you need them to be higher.

Doors and windows

My original cardboard box gallery had a door cut into it that was hinged by a fold. This was originally used as an access point to take photos but became very useful in private views because I could place a security guard next to it, giving me scope for loads of narrative about the visitors.

When you visit a gallery people come in and out all the time. Catching this mundane act in a tiny gallery gives it a sense of reality.

Windows bring scale and light. A floor to ceiling window has a modern feel to it.

Glass ceilings are reminiscent of Victorian galleries and give light without damaging the art.

Windows can just be holes in the walls, or you could add perspex, plastic, cling film or tissue paper. If you are only taking photos from the inside of the gallery, the outside can be a mess of tape and structural supports that no one will know about.

Props

For galleries that present a narrative, props come in very handy. The private views at the Tiny Cat Gallery are catered with small bowls of milk. I take a series of photos where the bowls move around, get shared, spilled, stood on and eventually emptied. This prop becomes part of the weird reality I'm creating.

Your gallery might need a donation box, signs for the loo, catalogues, postcards, souvenir mugs etc.

One visit to a real life art gallery will give you loads of ideas for props you can incorporate in your tiny gallery.

"**When** you take seriously what you create others start to believe in it too. It becomes public the same moment you show it."

Indrė Ercmonaitė, Mini Gallery Don't Cry

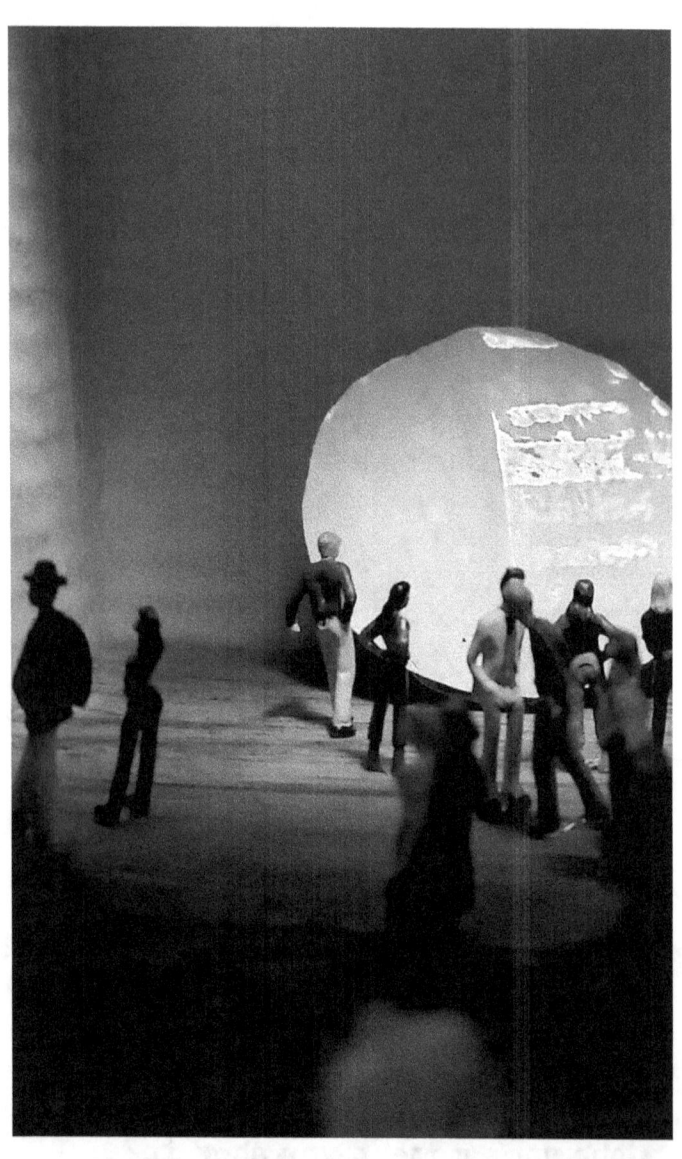

Ryan Boultbees at The Cardboard Monkey Gallery.

Enforcing Scale

Some galleries use their actual construction and location to give a sense of scale. My gallery happens to have 3cm tall plastic cats visiting and staffing it. The scale of the cats gives the human a sense of how the artwork might look in a full sized gallery. Without the cats there is nothing to tell the viewer what size anything is.

The small visitors to your gallery will dictate how large the artwork appears. You might be able to use the same gallery space with different scaled visitors.

Tiny visitors could include:

- Barbies/Cindy's/Action men/Kens
- Playmobil/Lego figures
- Dinosaurs/Model animals
- Toy soldiers
- 3D prints
- Architecture figures/Model railway figures
- Live animals; be very careful that pets are safe with artwork they might try to eat.

If you are not using figures to enforce scale what is there in your gallery environment that you can use? What point of reference are you using so that your human viewers know they are looking at a tiny gallery?

Photography and Storytelling

Galleries that cannot be physically visited will have to find another way to communicate exhibitions. This gives you the opportunity to use words and pictures to bring your gallery to life. The easiest way to share what you are doing is online. The internet also makes it pretty easy to share videos which can really breath life into a tiny gallery.

Thinking back to our two audiences, you can take photos from either point of view. Think about the eye-line of your tiny visitor from their height and take pictures of what they can see. Or, be a huge overlord and take pictures looking at the smaller scale visitors.

If you don't use models for scale what other clues can you give the human viewer about the size of the artwork?

We all know roughly how tall a skirting board is, or a house brick and you can use these types of things as backgrounds for your images to set scale.

If you are using tiny visitors this gives you scope to write about them. What are they doing in the gallery? Do they like the art? Are they wondering if the cafe is open?

Sometimes I give the tiny visitors a name and a bit of a back story. They might be sitting down for a rest because it is raining outside, worrying about how a date is going or getting up to mischief.

Curator or critic?

Personally I don't feel qualified to talk about the artwork critically. It can be tempting to write about art in a grandiose and/or comedic way. If you are writing about your own work, then fair game, wax lyrical about the postmodern dialectic (or whatever buzz words you have to hand).

If an artist has given you a pile of what you see as junk but they consider it to be art, it is art. Present it as such, please treat it with respect. Your job as a curator is not to critique but to promote and encourage.

Write from the heart about the artwork. Start with a basic description stating colours and layout. Is it abstract? Is it a photograph? Move onto how it makes you feel and it is quite OK to say you feel confused. Ideally the artist you are showing will have given you some text you can refer to so you have a better idea of the concepts behind artwork. If they haven't, you can either not talk about it, or be honest and kind in your comments.

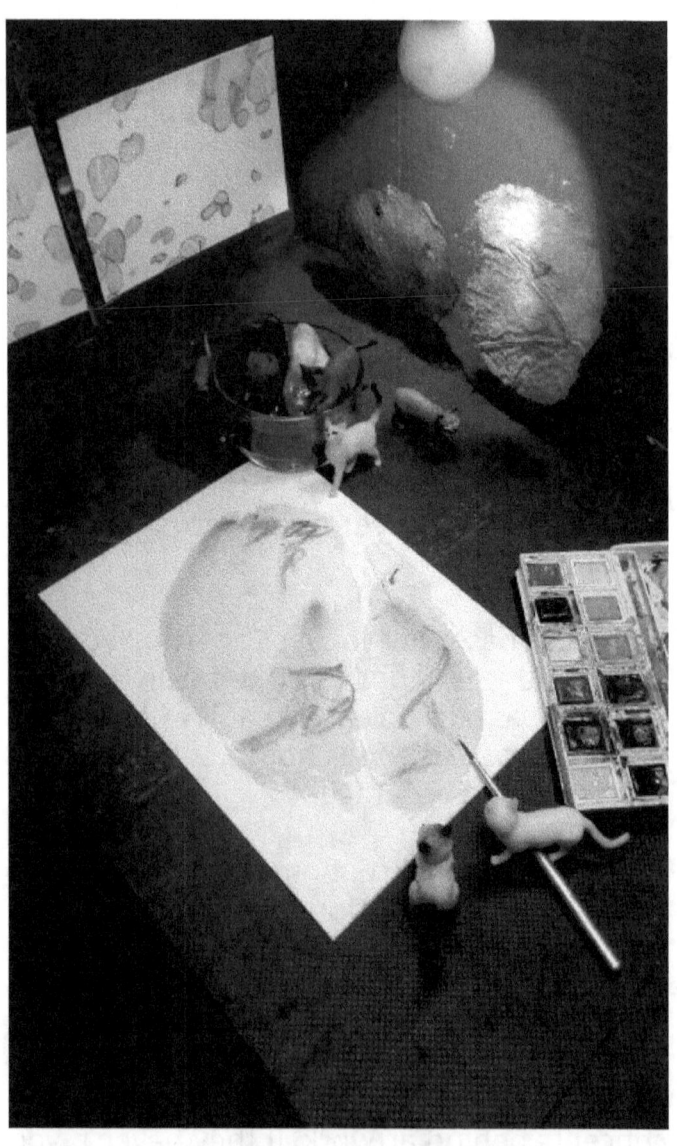

Watercolour workshop run by Lorraine Whelan for her 'Liminal' exhibition at the Tiny Cat Gallery.

Types of events

Exhibitions in real art galleries usually start with a private view or preview. This is often more about the people invited than the artwork and can be a catered lavish affair with music and important people.

There is no reason why you couldn't live stream a private view to a selected audience using video meeting software. If you are doing that there will be some challenges to make it interesting and you may want to talk about the artwork as you film it.

You can put on a show with your own work or other artists as a solo show or group exhibitions. Group exhibitions work well for promotion because all the artists can share what is happening with their individual networks.

Workshops themed around exhibitions work well on social media. Share a video of an activity, or provide a worksheet and ask participants to post their results and tag you.

This system works for educational trips to your gallery and can be supplemented with an artists talk.

"When working with artists as a curator, do not assume anything, you are there to guide and support them and to help bring their vision to life."

Sally Eldars, The Open Dresser Gallery

Curating

Working with Artists

A tiny gallery allows you to experiment with very little risk and put on exhibitions from different types of artists. One week might be a series of landscapes, the next might be abstract sculpture.

Each artist brings new and often delightful challenges but clear communications will always help things go more smoothly. After you have seen the artists work, and talked to them about the kind of show they want to put on make sure that you are both clear about how it will work.

Have you agreed:

- The title and contents of the exhibition
- How long the show will run for
- How the work will be fixed to walls
- If the work will be framed
- How the work will be lit
- How it will be promoted
- If work is to be sold, prices and commission
- How work is to be packaged if sold
- The logistics of selling, who posts it, how will it be shipped, when will payment be sent.
- How long you will keep work for after the exhibition
- How artwork will be returned to the artist
- If the artwork is insured and by whom

Artists details

This is the basic information you will need from each artist.

- Name
- Artists name if different
- Collective name if applicable
- Address
- Website/Instagram etc.
- Email
- Phone number
- Method of payment

Exhibition details

What really helps here are snippets of information that you can cut and paste into social media posts. The artist will know their work better than anyone, let them speak about it using quote marks. Gather this information to make your life easier. Answer questions about who, what, where, why and when so you cover all bases. You may need to proof read, edit and get approval for changes.

- Title of show
- Abstract of proposal — what is it about?
- Proposal — a longer version of what it is about and how it is done.
- Artists bio — what they have done before
- Artists statement — why they do what they do

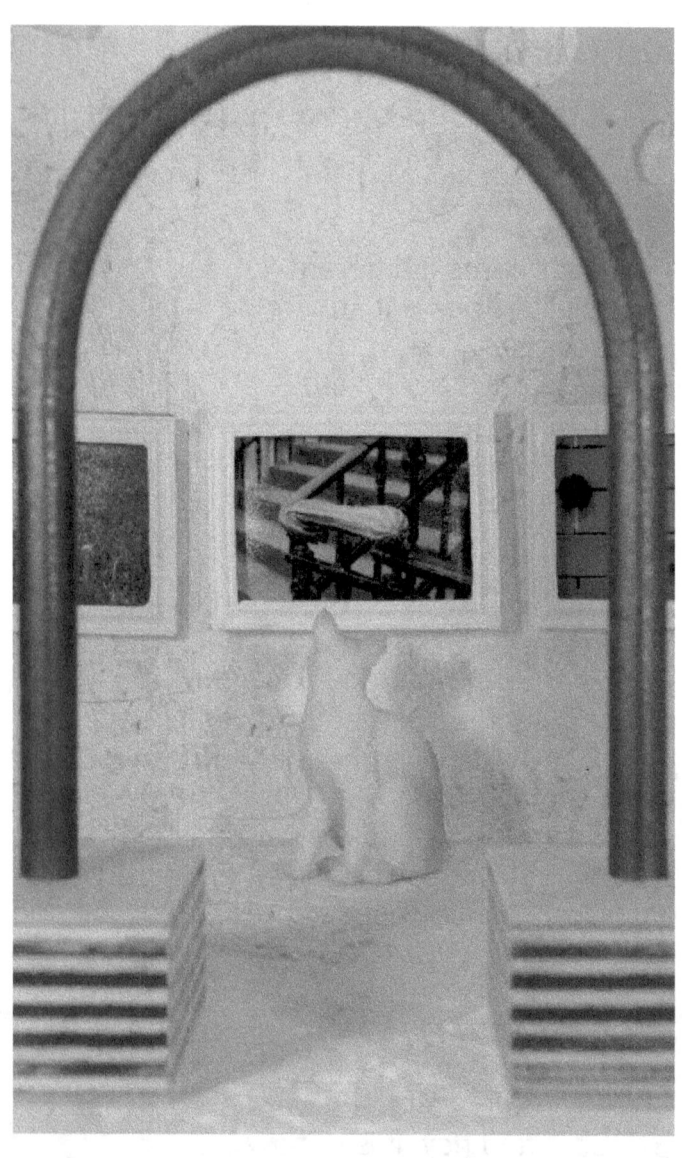

'An Exhibition for Mice' by Amy J Grogan at the Tiny Cat Gallery.

Artwork details

For each artwork you need to know these details

- Title
- Dimensions (length x height x depth)
- Materials and method
- Is it original or part of a limited run?
- Year completed

Artwork images

Ask your artists to send you good quality images of their work for your shop and also for you to post in case it is hard to see their work in your gallery.

For the internet you won't need images larger than 1600px, anything bigger will slow down a website.

Ask your artists to optimise them which squashes down the file to make it take up less space while still retaining physical size.

It really helps if they save artwork in a format that helps you recognise it.

Use this format:
Artist name — Artwork name — Length x Height x Depth — Year

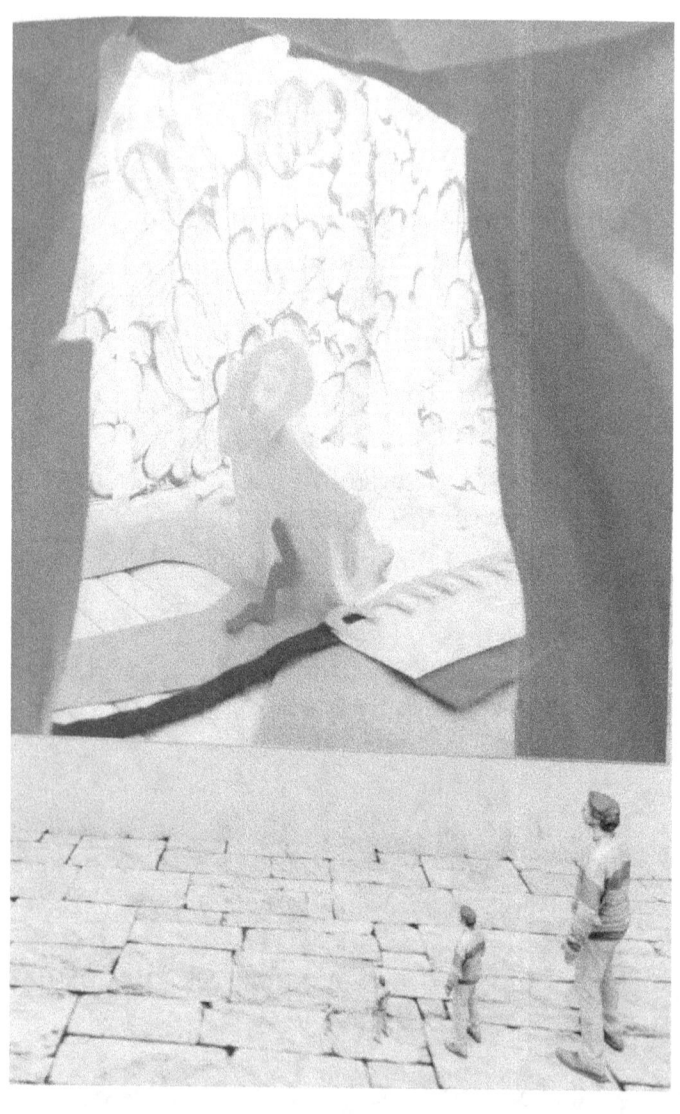

'A Degree Show For Ants' 2020, by artist Jody Mulvey.

Digital image of actual sculpture mounted on virtual canvas hung in Groock's Gallery.

Maintain curatorial control

If, despite checking and agreeing with your artist, they send you something unexpected remember it is your gallery. As a last resort you can pull the show and simply not run it. It probably won't come to that as long as expectations are managed.

I've had a couple of artists who didn't understand the limitations of a tiny gallery and sent me artwork to fill all 4 walls, not realising that one wall had to be folded back so I could take photos. That is easily remedied by leaving some artwork out and you can negotiate that with the artist.

Framing or giving flat artworks depth by mounting on foam board can make a huge difference. Have a look at a few real life size galleries and you will notice that it is very rare to have paper blue tacked to a wall. Prints and drawings are generally framed and canvases have depth to them.

It might be interesting to play around with these conventions but to make your gallery more believable, stick to what people are used to seeing. A postcard of an old master displayed in an ornate frame will read very differently to one stuck straight on the wall.

"**Good administration is key, there's an art to it.**"

George Thom, Groock's Gallery

Commerce

Making Money

Even if your gallery is 'just a hobby', making money out of it will help you continue to run and to grow it.

You can establish your tiny gallery as an alternative reality that functions in it's own normality by running it along the same lines as a real life commercial gallery.

It is normal for commercial galleries to take a commission on sales between 30% and 50%. This may or may not include postage and packing of orders and has to be factored in when pricing work.

You can dictate how you want this to work, or you can ask the artist to tell you the amount they want for each artwork and add your commission to make it into a viable price.

Pricing is always difficult, test it out, see what the market will bear and don't be afraid to put the prices up, people tend not to trust cheap things.

It can be tempting to use your own gallery as a comment on the high prices art can fetch by pricing your shows at thousands or millions of pounds.

You are unlikely to sell anything at all if you do that, but you could try pricing a main work at a million and selling a diffusion line of more affordable works.

The type of work that consistently sells in my gallery is by artists who normally work at a larger scale. The art buying public seem to like the idea of having a small work by someone who may become collectable. It also allows people who do not have much wall space to exhibit artwork.

Other galleries do better selling work that is specifically miniature by artists who specialise in small work.

You can make money by selling your own work, selling artists work, selling merchandise and gift shop items. I get as much of a buzz out of selling someone else's work as I do selling my own.

> "People who look at art are in general very curious. They don't like cheating. You can't cheat about art, because it is a very vulnerable subject."
> Indrė Ercmonaitė. Mini Gallery Don't Cry

Marketing on Social Media

Social media platforms are designed to make money for themselves, so be aware that it is very difficult, even with tens of thousands of followers to get anyone to click through to a link to visit a website. However, social media is free and the only way that most of us have to promote our galleries.

You probably don't need a presence on all platforms. Think about what you want to get out of it, likes? chit chat? sales?

If you have no social media accounts at all concentrate on just one that you think will work best for you. I've focused on the main ones here that I'm confident will stick around for the next few years.

You can use external resources to schedule posts on most social media platforms. This means you can do all the work as a batch and not be tied up with it all the time.

Facebook

Good for group conversations and for building communities in a way that people feel safe. You start with a Profile that you can make private.

For a business, or if you want your shop to be on Facebook you need a Page and if your gallery has a focus on a cause, a Facebook group might be a good place for people to talk about it. You can put as many words as you like on a Facebook post and you can share multiple images at once or videos. You can also do live shows.

Instagram

A visual storytelling platform best for sharing images and videos. You are not limited in your word count and you can use hashtags so that you show up in other peoples searches. You can do live shows here and your followers will get a notification in the App when you are live.

Facebook and Instagram are related and interlinked and you can set things in your Instagram settings so that Posts and stories on Instagram show up on your Facebook page. This saves you time as you can just focus on Instagram knowing that Facebook is taking care of itself.

"**Fake art is drowning all the subtleties to the bottom. Mini Gallery Don't Cry exhibits art.**"

Indrė Ercmonaitė, Mini Gallery Don't Cry

Twitter

With limited word counts that include hashtags you have to be concise on Twitter. You can share images and videos and it is pretty straightforward to get other platforms to post to Twitter automatically.

Pinterest

Image based platform that is great for storing and organising interests in a visual way.

You can make boards with topics and save images to them. Pinterest shows you new things based on what you have saved.

Pinterest could be a good platform for tiny galleries because it is so visual. Be sure to check the automatically created title and description of images you pin so that people can find you.

Facebook, Instagram, Twitter and Pinterest are the main players in social media at the time of writing. TikTok is becoming more popular with a younger audience and streaming platform Twitch is moving forwards from computer games into art and craft. Both these are worth exploring but consider your target audience and establish a presence where they hang out.

Gaining followers

Start by following people you know well because they are most likely to follow you back. Then move onto following people who's work you like. Find other small galleries to follow and join in with any sharing hashtags they might be using — like #MicroGalleryMonday where we all repost what each other is up to.

Be nice to people. Ask questions, compliment other galleries, respond to comments and generally be a lovely person if you want your gallery to be shared.

You can follow hashtags as well as accounts which lets you keep an eye on new galleries as they come up. Some might over take you with followers so be nice to them on their way up.

Invent awards and give them out, even if they are ultimately meaningless and something you decided to do on a whim. Who wouldn't want to win a tiny gallery of the week award?

> **"Duly credit all the work, spread positivity and you will be rewarded with positivity."**
> George Thom, Grooks Gallery

Hashtags

Hashtags are searchable words that always start with # and never have any gaps. They are not fussy about letter case so you can use capitals but remember all caps is considered shouting online.

The large umbrella terms are going to be used by more people and the smaller niche terms by less so it is a good idea to have a mixture.

Start big and narrow down. Instagram lets you have 30 hashtags so devote 10 to large descriptive terms:
#artgallery #artshow #artexhibition #fineart #artlovers #artforsale #soloshow #artist #modernart #contemporaryart

and 10 to specific tags.
#smallgallery #tinygallery #microgallery #cardboardboxgallery #artinabox #smallmodernart #minaturegallery #microart #smalldogpainting #miniart

Fit the remaining tags somewhere in between.

Alternatives to social media

If you are not bothered by the amount of people you engage with but you still want your gallery to be online consider a free blog before investing in a website.

WordPress and Medium both have free levels but watch WordPress for the upsells and make sure you tick all the free options.

There are many other platforms but it is safest to stick with a long standing one. A fairy dies every time someone makes a Wix site. Please don't be a fairy killer. (More practically they tend to look bad on phones and they don't perform well in searches).

If you want things to look more professional buy a domain name and point it at either your Instagram/Facebook or at your free blog. This means that you can give out your website address and people will go straight to where you are active.

You can always move onto a website devoted to your gallery later on if you need to.

"I love giving opportunities to new artists as well as established names."

Sam Toft, Dog and Bone Gallery

Case Studies

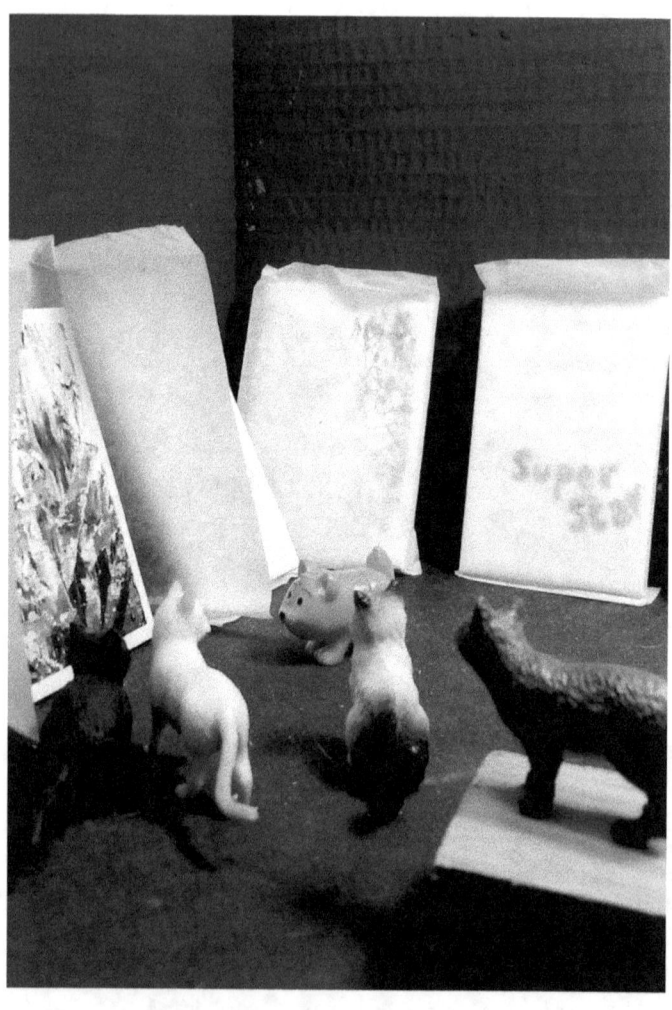

Tiny technicians setting up 'Retrospective' by Philip Ryland at the Tiny Cat Gallery.

Ryland's work was sent mounted on foam board and individually wrapped in tissue paper.

The Tiny Cat Gallery

Originally a cardboard box, currently a 23 cm cubed wooden box.

www.tcgallery.co.uk or www.lisa-cole.co.uk
Instagram: @tiny.cat.gallery

Why did you open a tiny gallery?

The Tiny Cat Gallery started with an art exchange as an experiment in scale.

Artist Lizzie Don posted me some of her work to display in my home to a tiny lockdown audience of a couple of humans and a pair of cats. I wanted to see how her A4 sized collages would work if they took up a whole wall so I painted a cardboard box and hung them up.

Adding plastic cats seemed an obvious move after that. The cats define the scale and your brain immediately makes the art much bigger than it is in real life.

What do you exhibit?

I have an open call for light hearted exhibitions but I don't have any themes at the moment.

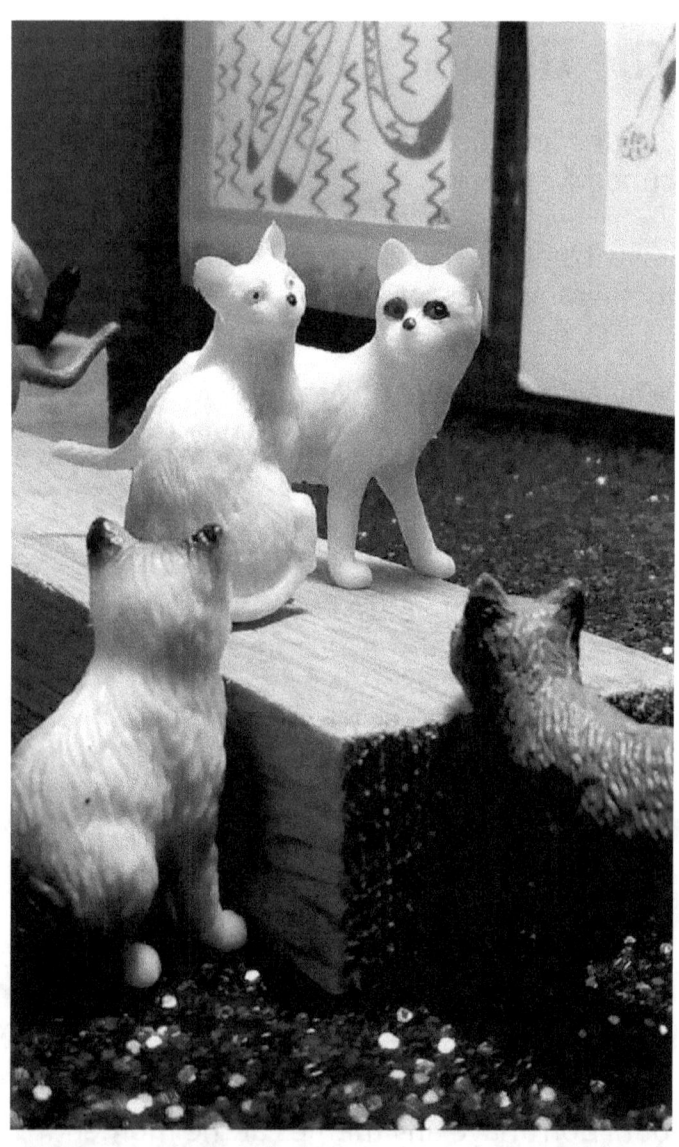

At the private view for 'Cat a Day' by Jo Coffey at the Tiny Cat Gallery

What do you wish you had known before you opened your gallery?

That it would take over my life. My first season ran back to back exhibitions for eight weeks and I had no time to do any creative work of my own. Now I have a week off in between exhibitions and I take all the images in one day so I can schedule them to appear throughout the week. That saves lots of time but I still need to be on hand to respond to comments.

What is the best thing about running a tiny gallery?

The thrill of selling someone's work is incredible and just as invigorating as selling my own work. I've learned an incredible amount from working with different artists and exhibiting in challenging tiny spaces.

What advice would you give someone starting a tiny gallery?

Firstly, ask the artists you exhibit to share mercilessly on social media. It makes a huge difference to the success of a show if your artists are engaged and respond to comments.

Secondly, buy this book. Buy lots of copies of this book and give it to all your friends.

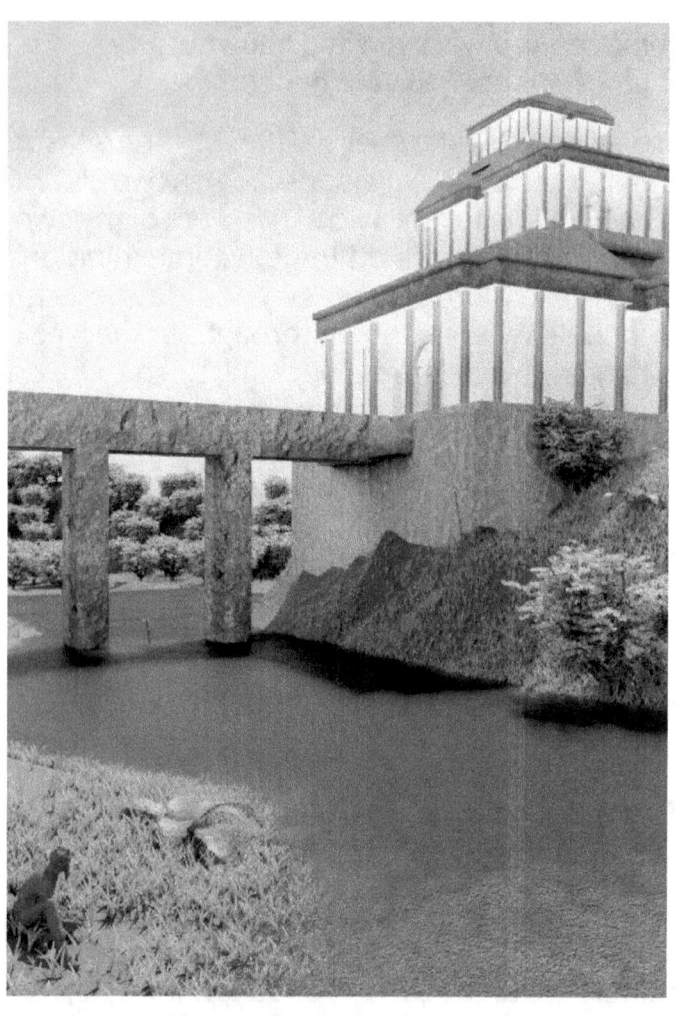

The exterior of Groock's Gallery.

www.groocksgallery.com has been host to a range of different virtual exhibitions, all navigable by the viewer/user using a keyboard and mouse.

Groock's Gallery

Interactive and virtual gallery
www.groocksgallery.com
Instagram: @groocksgallery

Groock's Gallery being a tiny gallery that exists in the microchips on my computer is probably much less than 1mm square. But being a digital gallery, it extends itself into other dimensions.

One example is a live-streamed virtual tour of an exhibition for the Art Car Boot Fair, with exhibiting artists, Ian Dawson, Annette Warner, James Hewins and George Thom. Streamed on the 4th October 2020.

Another dimension of Groock's being the interactive website, accessible from a laptop or desktop computer.

Why did you open a tiny gallery?

It just kind of happened, I had already made a virtual world, so making a virtual gallery while I was studying my 3rd year of my BA in Fine Art in 2016 just seemed like the right step to take.

I'm a big fan of collaborative projects and am interested in collaborative artists such as Joseph Beuys and Thomas Hirschhorn.

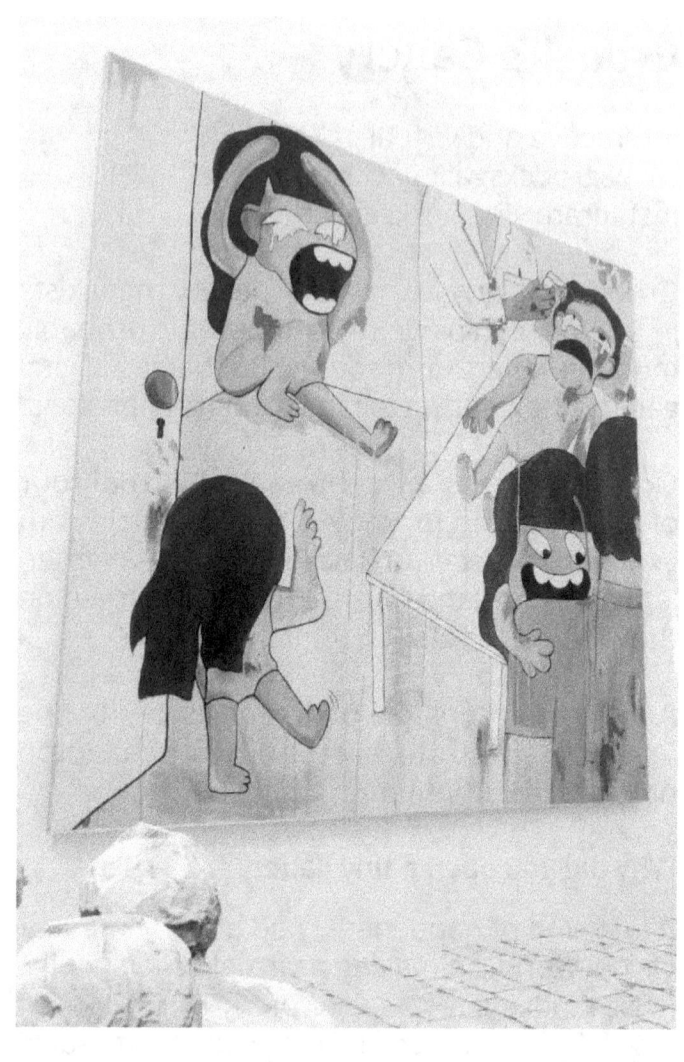

'Bumped My Head' by artist Bianca Schmittmann.

Digital image of actual painted work mounted on virtual canvas hung in Groock's Gallery.

I'm also inspired by the land artist Robert Smithson, I can see the landscaping coming through in some of the exterior shots of the gallery itself.

What do you exhibit?

Mostly images, some virtual sculpture, video and text pieces. Also the odd performative live stream here and there.

What do you wish you had known before you opened your gallery?

How much work it was going to be! haha.

What is the best thing about running a tiny gallery?

Seeing new art every day from wonderful artists around the world.

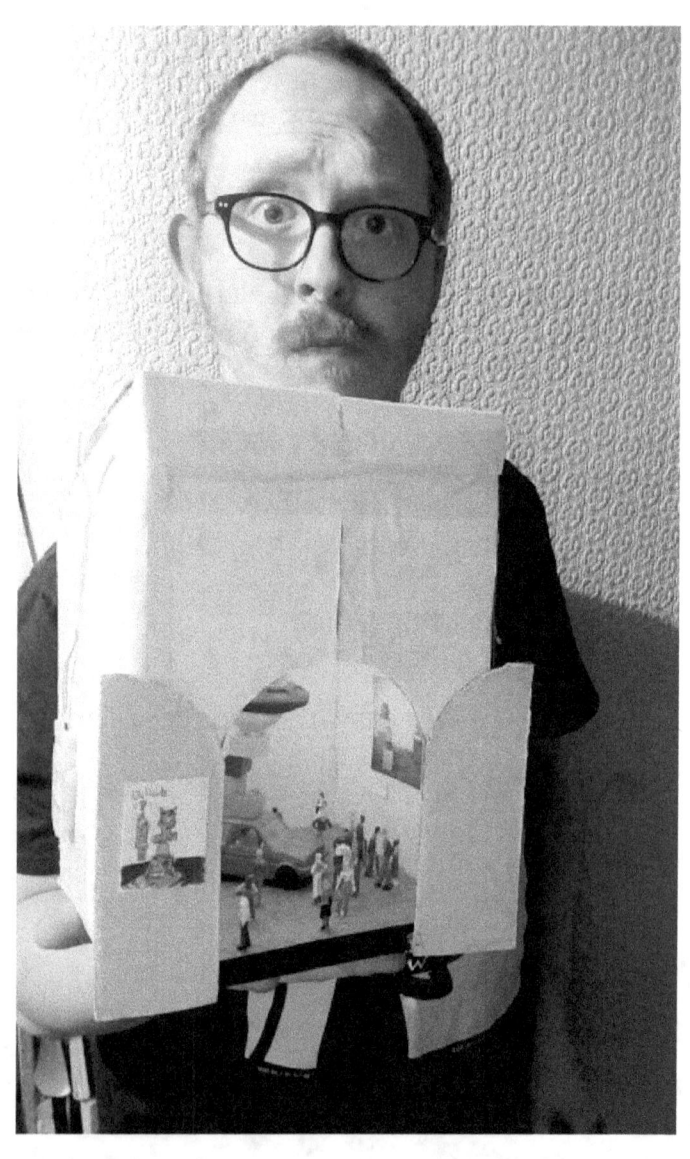

Jack Woodward and Cardboard Monkey Gallery.

Cardboard Monkey Gallery (C.B.M)

www.acardboardmonkey.com/cbm-galleries
Instagram: @acardboardmonkey

Why did you open a tiny gallery?

I decided to open C.B.M galleries whilst on a residency after being unable to make a larger version with the aim to exhibit students work, in those coveted areas that people want to show. I decided a miniature version that just works was the way to go.

What do you exhibit?

Everything including the kitchen sink. But typically work by students and emerging artists.

As the saying goes if it fits it sits and that's the approach I try and take with what I exhibit.

What do you wish you had known before you opened your gallery?

That no matter how clear you make the instructions or guidelines for people to follow there will be those who still can't grasp the scale of the gallery.

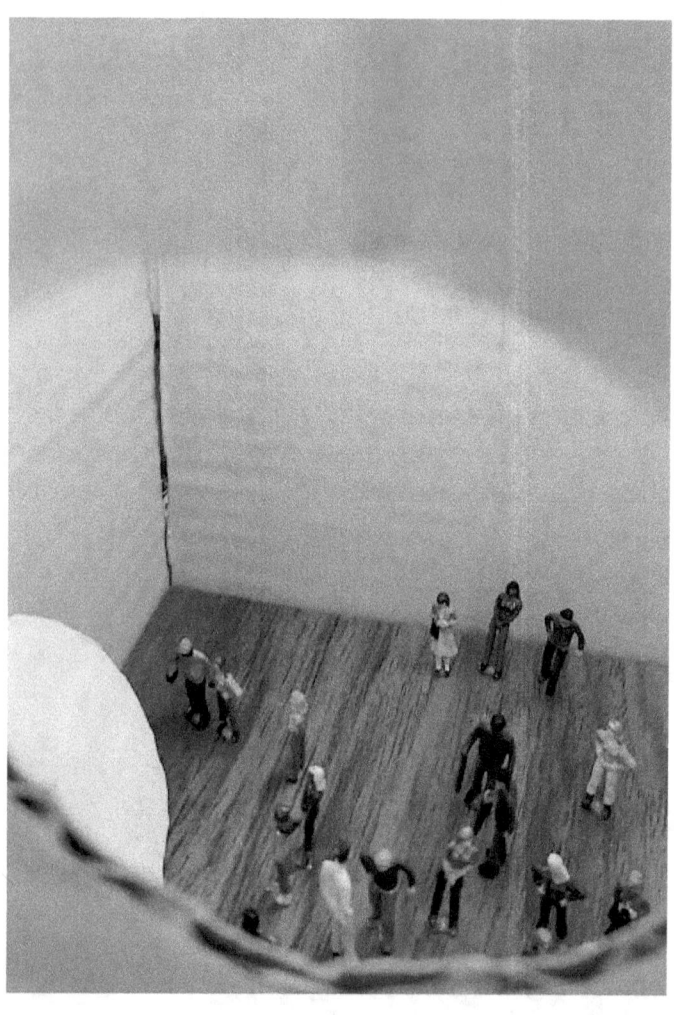

Ryan Boultbees at Cardboard Monkey Gallery (C.B.M).

The figures are 00 gauge plastic railway miniatures. Jack Woodward said "They are cheap and look rough but do the job. They are roughly an inch tall so it makes the 18 x 15 cm space look huge."

Also make sure that you can easily photograph / video all the works, it's a real pain when you just can't get a good picture of one piece.

What is the best thing about running a tiny gallery?

You get to exhibit peoples work, short cut the networking faff as people speak to you instead, have a couple different job rolls for the old CV and it makes you feel like a giant.

What advice would you give someone starting a tiny gallery?

Get yourself something to give scale to the work and add sense of life to the gallery. This can be tiny people, cats or even paper clips and pen tops with googly eyes.

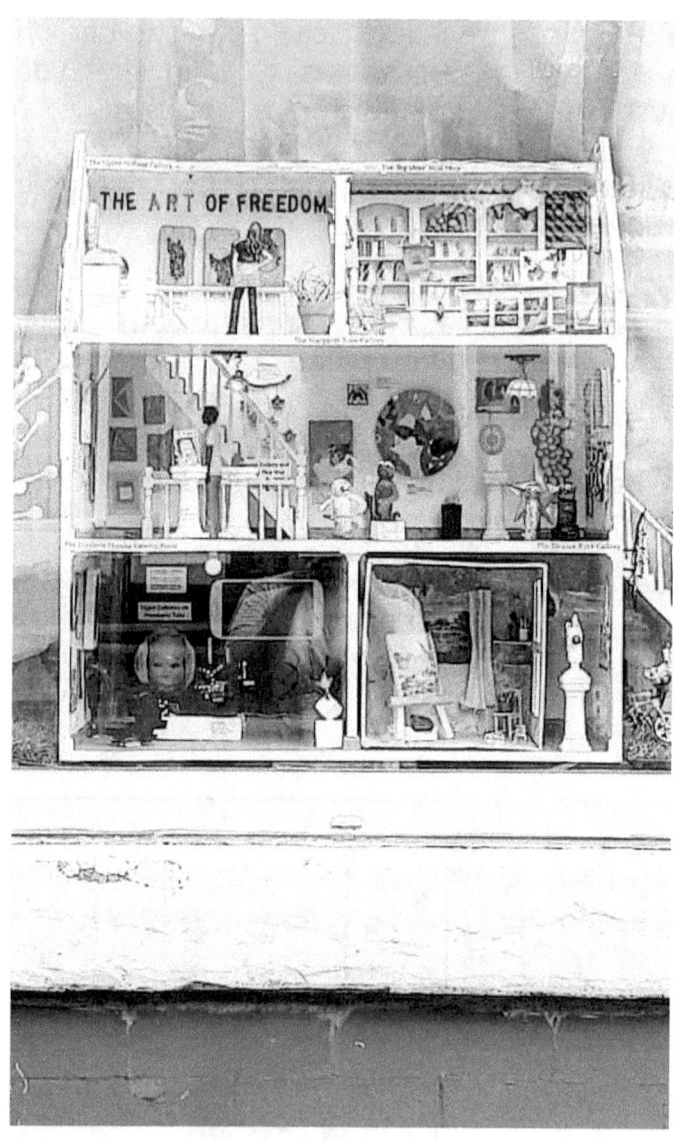

The Doll's House Art Gallery

The Doll's House Art Gallery

Multiple rooms inside a doll's house displayed in a residential window in Manchester, UK.

Instagram: @thedollshouseartgallery

Why did you open a tiny gallery?

At first I wanted to open a tiny gallery because of my love of miniature.

I work in a full-sized art gallery and visit them frequently, I create miniature art myself and have previously created window displays. Also, having enjoyed (and finished) renovating an heirloom doll's house made by my grandfather and left to me by my mother, I felt I wanted to start another project.

I bought a doll's house, but life interfered and I didn't have the motivation for it until the pandemic began. In March 2020, I decided that I needed to force myself to take on a (at least in part) offline creative project that connects people.

I wanted it to make me smile, and others too. I also hoped it could be a way to inspire and promote artists and locals during a difficult time.

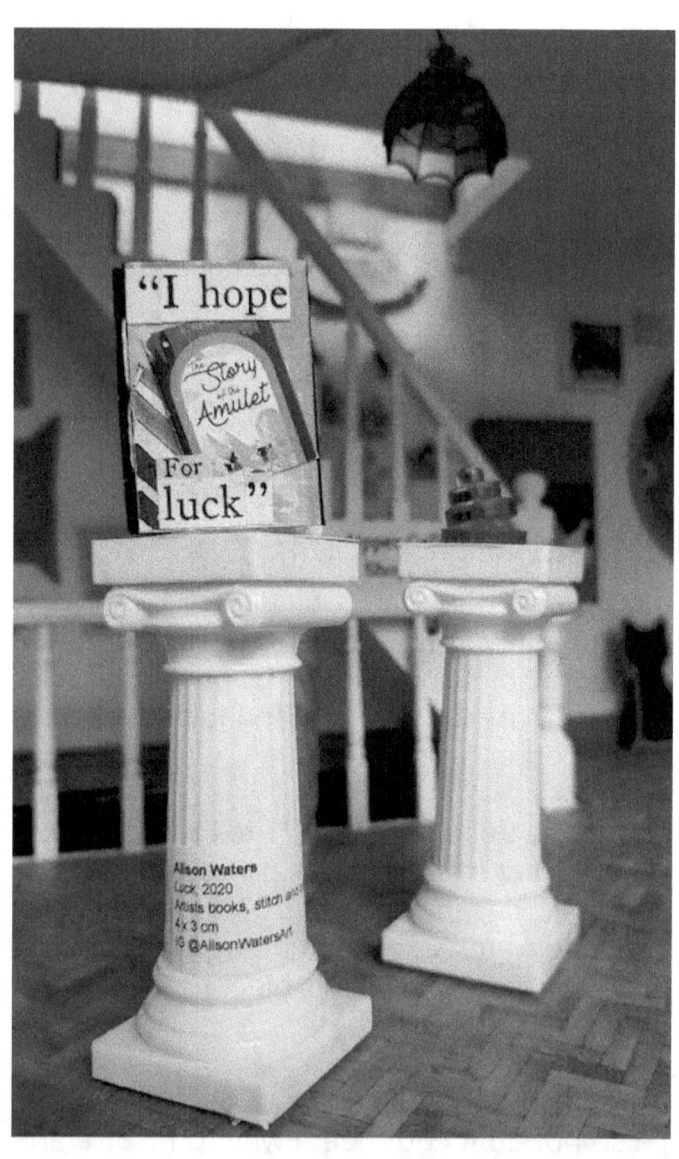

Alison Waters at The Doll's House Art Gallery.

What do you exhibit?

As of October 2020 the gallery is exhibiting artwork received after an open call.

Pieces were sent to us by people from mostly Manchester, around the UK, and even Texas, USA!

It is a varied mix of work from photography and video to sculpture, paintings and craft. There is also a mini 'shop' of tiny home-wares and stationery.

As the gallery is currently in a bay window, its future could be for it to get its own perspex frontage and then house further opens, solo exhibitions, seek local business partnerships, run related workshops, tour other venues and possibly earn money as a not-for-profit artist space.

It would be great to enable organisations to use their imaginations to promote their work within it.

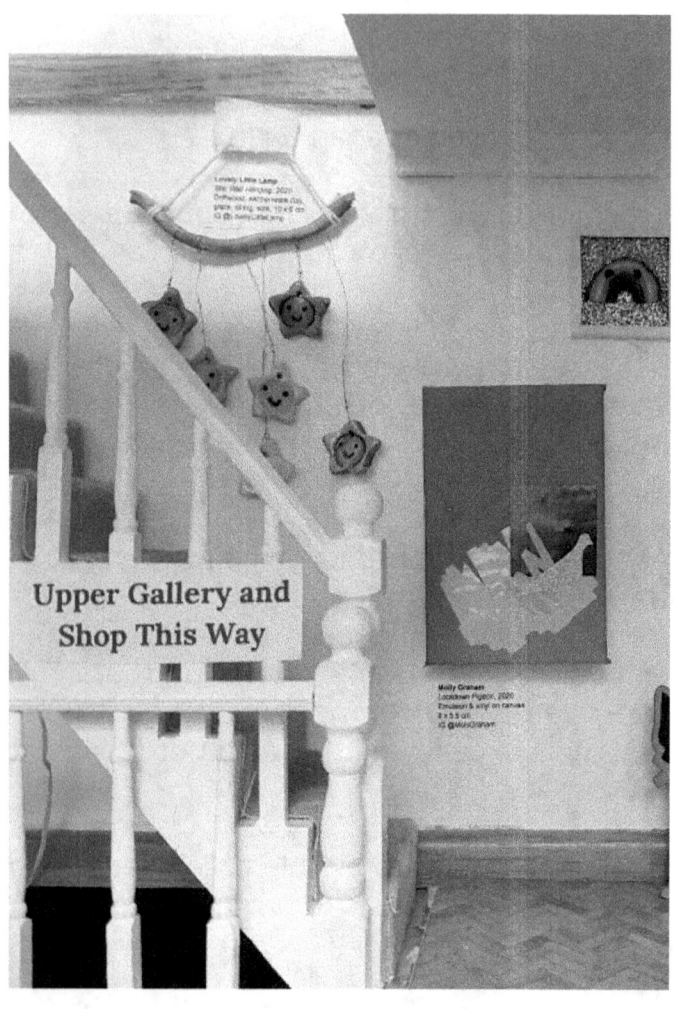

Signposting at The Doll's House Art Gallery leading viewers past artwork by Lovely Little Lamp and Molly Graham.

What do you wish you had known before you opened your gallery?

That curating a tiny exhibition isn't actually much less work and time than a full-sized one!
There is quite a bit of time for admin and marketing required too.

And always remove patterned wallpaper before painting it white!

What is the best thing about running a tiny gallery?

Providing a safe and engaging activity during a time when people are mostly housebound has been quite rewarding, seeing local people tag their friends and get excited about it online.

Hearing whoops of delight and awe, I think the fact that the art is miniature is particularly impressive to 'non-artists', and children and dreamers are enchanted by the miniature aspect alone.

I am really happy to have been able to bring art to my community of Levenshulme when many venues have been forced to close.

Also just getting to look at tiny art; what's better really, other than tiny cats looking at tiny art?

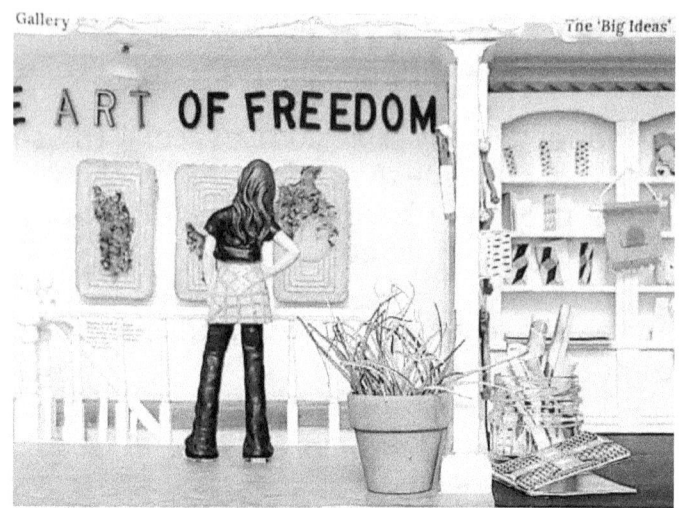

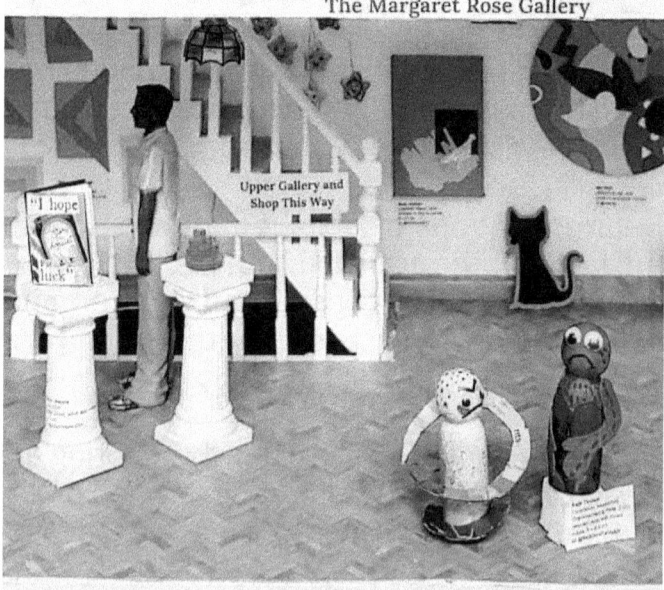

Multiple exhibition spaces at The Doll's House Art Gallery.

What advice would you give someone starting a tiny gallery?

It's a good idea to troubleshoot your 'business' model! Do a risk assessment and have systems in place.

Be passionate about it. If you're not and it's going to fizzle immediately, wait until you are!

Do your research and have a unique style and story that captures people's imaginations.

I think it's fine to want to include your own work, but don't just do it for yourself... Inspire, engage, have fun!

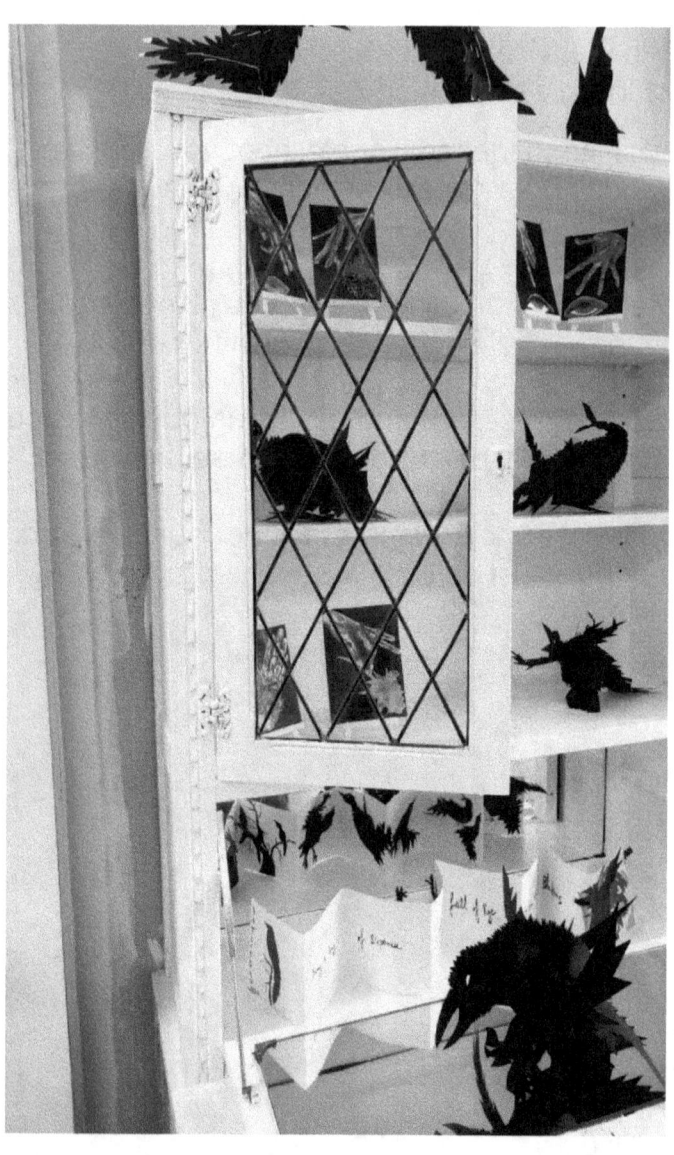

'4&Twenty' by Marie-Therese Ross at TOD Gallery.

The Open Dresser (TOD) Gallery

The gallery runs out of a wooden dresser with glass doors and a pull down mirrored shelf.

todgallery.com
Instagram: @theopendressergallery

Why did you open a tiny gallery?
Started as a lockdown project after all art events, open studios and gallery were closed, to reach out to other artists and audiences via social media.

What do you exhibit?

We particularly exhibit artists that focus on and examine identity, gender, mental health, socio-politics, cultural or environmental issues in their work.

What do you wish you had known before you opened your gallery?

More knowledge on how to use social media, and that it is almost a full-time job if you want to run the gallery as professional as possible.

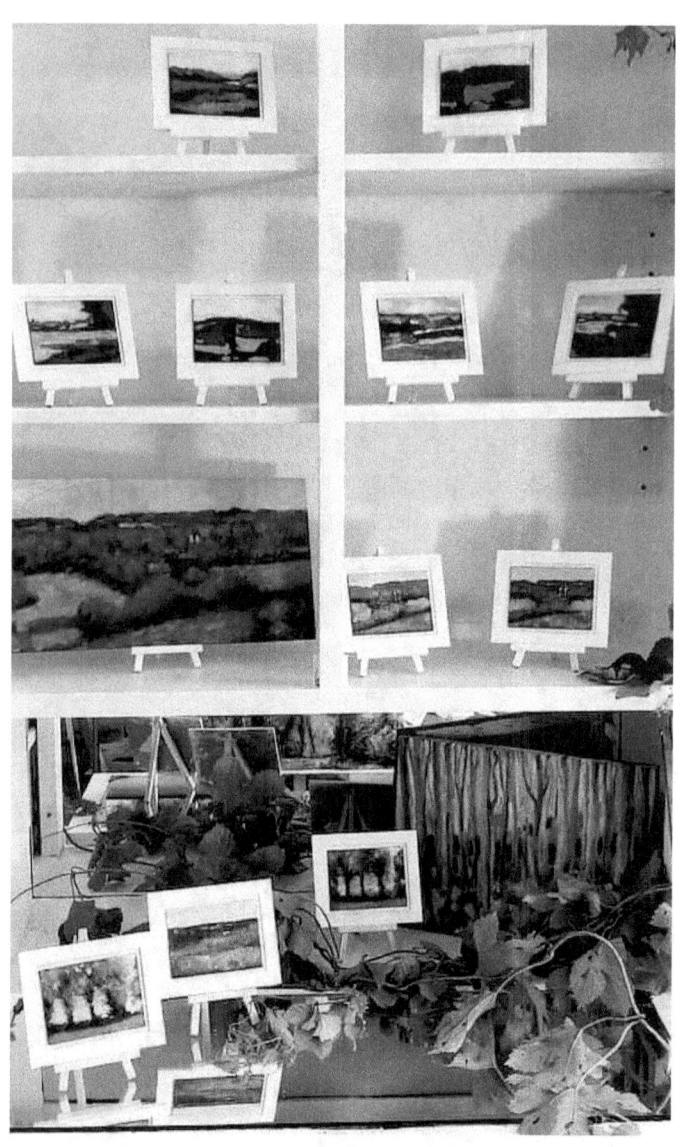

'After' by Mike Roberts at TOD Gallery.

What is the best thing about running a tiny gallery?

Meeting like minded artists and networking which is then reflected back into my own practice.

Giving artists a space where they can show and develop their work and ideas.

Contributing to the growing online visual art community.

Learning and developing my curatorial skills.

What advice would you give someone starting a tiny gallery?

Start small (a shelf or a box) but be ambitious and take it serious. A cardboard box can be just as professional as a traditional white box gallery.

Don't be shy, reach out to other curators of unconventional galleries online and ask for help and advice.

Brush up on your IT and social media skills.

Have very clear terms and conditions, especially if you will be selling the artwork.

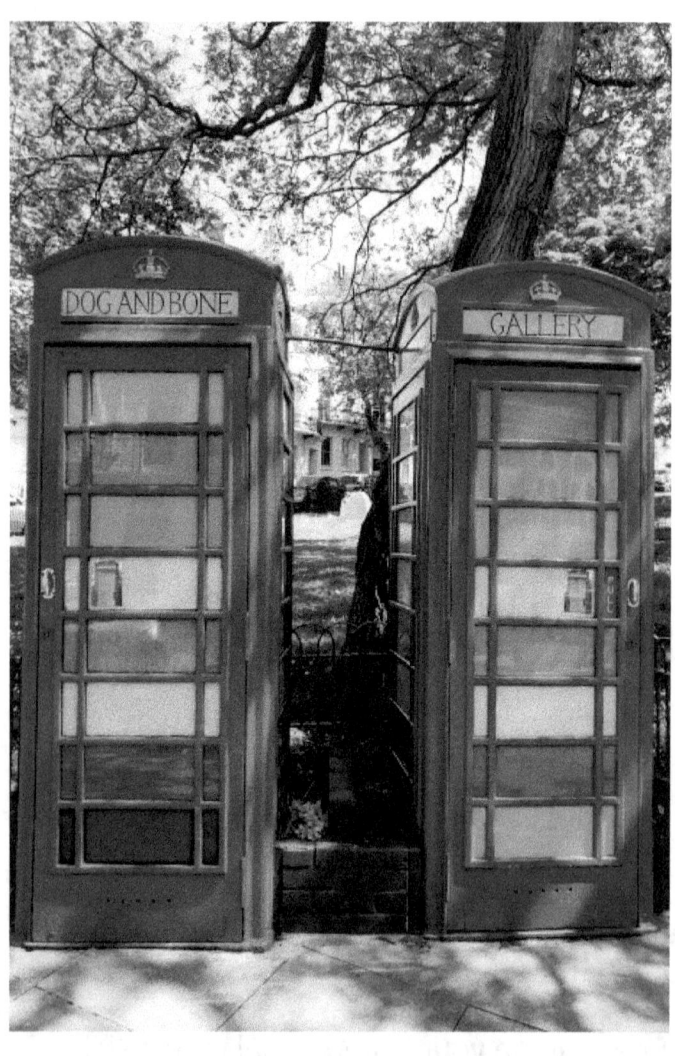

During the first COVID lockdown Amber Honess created this work at the Dog & Bone Gallery painting directly onto the glass panels to create a stunning rainbow installation (especially good at night as it is lit from within).

The Dog & Bone Gallery

Two phone boxes in Brighton, England.
Instagram: @dogandbonegallery

Why did you open a tiny gallery?

About three years ago I opened a little shop in Brighton and around the corner in a pretty Georgian square stood two neglected red phone boxes. I probably would not have noticed them if my head wasn't full of the joy of starting a new business. But the thought of renovating the boxes and having them as a community gallery space suddenly seemed extremely appealing.

I had seen phone boxes run as book swaps and coffee shops but never as a gallery, and without much thought I decided to give it a go. First I rented them and spent my own time and money restoring them and commissioning new signs.

Instead of the missing TELEPHONE signs we added DOG & BONE GALLERY. The insides too were in a terrible state having probably been used as a urinal for years. I installed new locks, panelled over the loose wires at the back, painted the interiors a dark charcoal grey, replaced graffitied glass panels, planted the little area around the boxes with bulbs and perennials: a true labour of love.

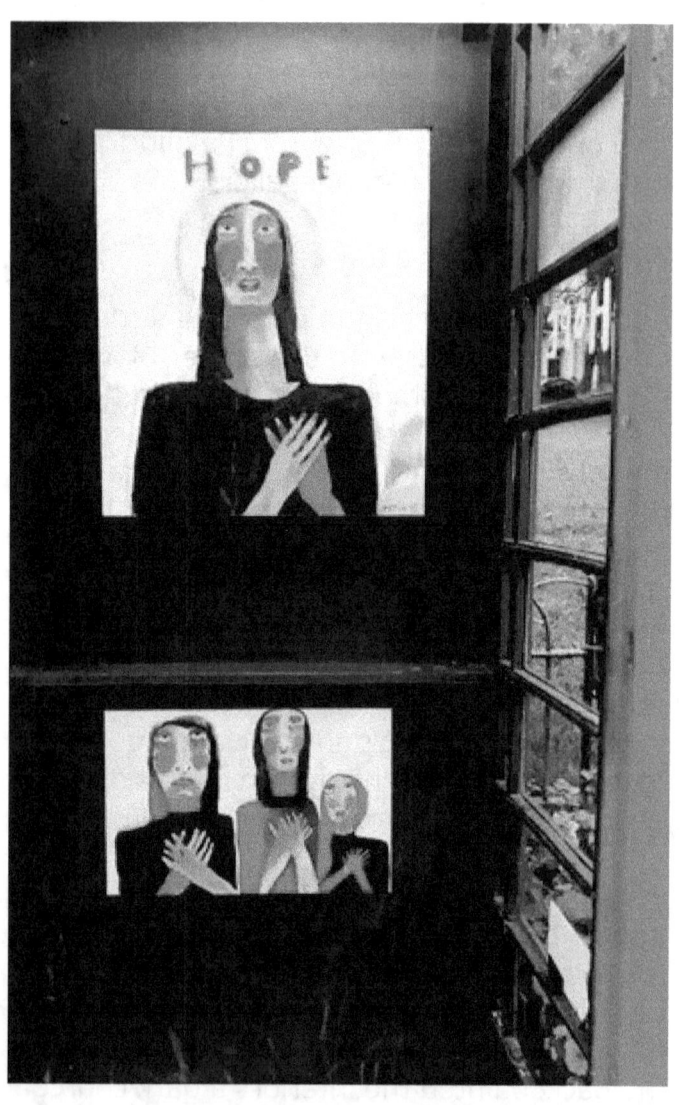

'Hope' by Sophie Wake at the Dog & Bone Gallery.

Visually arresting and such a strong message for the community in times of lockdown.

What do you exhibit?

From the beginning I knew that I wanted to run the gallery as a non profit making business. And I don't get involved in sales at all. I promote via an Instagram account and direct any queries direct to the artist.

My initial thought was to run the boxes as two separate exhibition spaces and firstly for ease I approached friends to invite them to hang their work. Brighton is full of artists and there are so few exhibition spaces.

Hanging two monthly shows became too much work, so I decided to have one artist at a time using both spaces.

I am proud to run Dog & Bone as free, open submission gallery space. At first using mostly local artists, but as we gain popularity there are submissions from further afield.

What do you wish you had known before you opened your gallery?

It surprised me how much work was involved. Weekly upkeep, dealing with enquiries, going through submissions, managing the social media. And the expense of dealing with graffiti and vandalism. I sometimes need to remind myself of the initial dream.

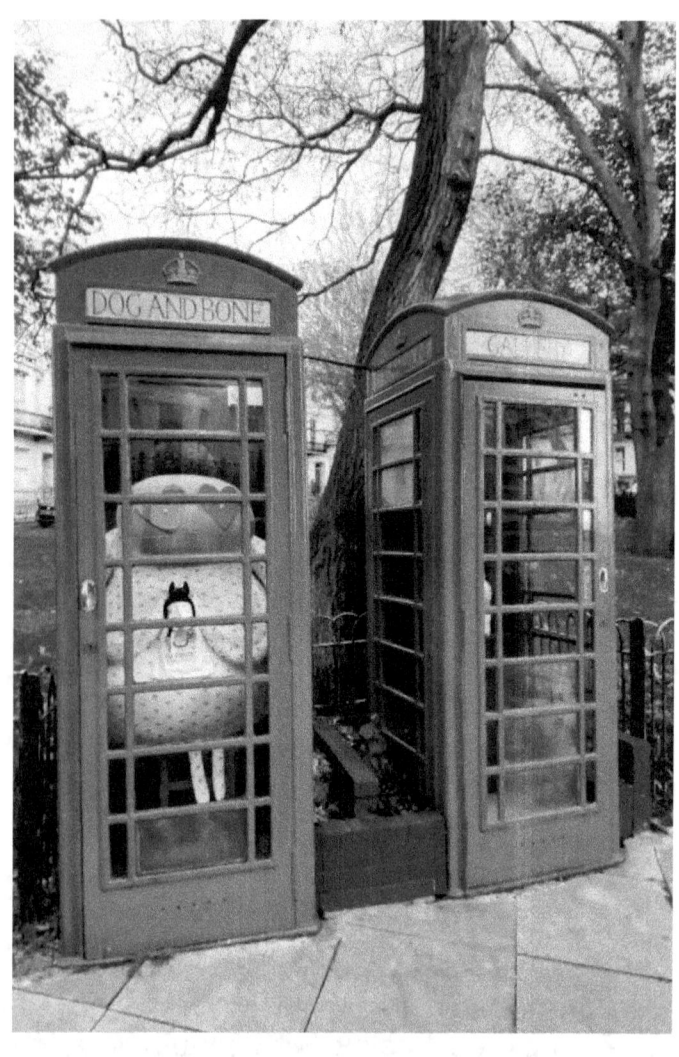

Ron and Jasper in 'Black Cat Magic', a stunning show by Jenny Mustill at the Dog & Bone Gallery.

Big Ron was made especially and is a perfect fit.

And to remember that it is truly worth while creating something quirky and beautiful for no other reason than to promote art in the community and to bring a smile to strangers' faces.

What is the best thing about running a tiny gallery?

Now that I have bought the phone boxes rather than renting them, I feel like I am really building something. I love it when artists create site specific work and paint directly onto the panels.

And I love seeing passers by stop and peer inside, knowing that if it weren't for me, quite possibly the boxes would be derelict, or selling coffee.

What advice would you give someone starting a tiny gallery?

Go for it. Dream big. Be the person who has a vision and sees it through. Get help. Keep positive. Believe that art in all its forms has the power to transform lives on so many levels.

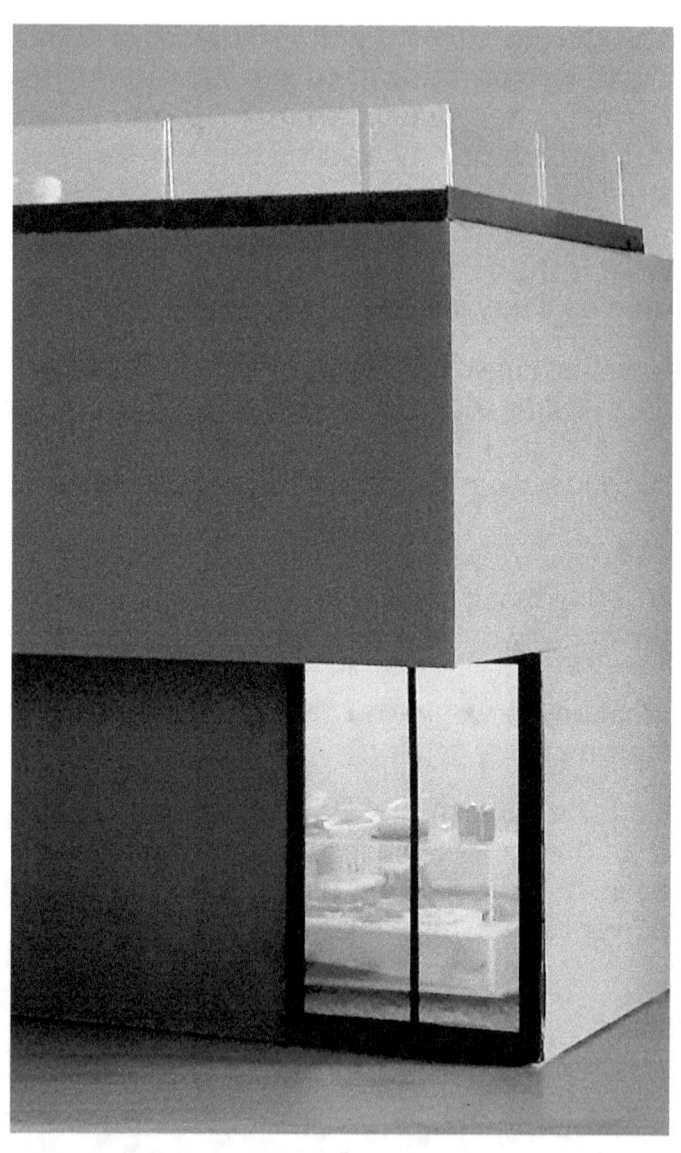

Beyond Scale gallery, exterior view.

Beyond Scale

Model gallery purpose built.
beyondscale.wordpress.com
Instagram: #beyondscalegallery

Why did you open a tiny gallery?

I have always loved miniatures and doll-houses and scale is something very important in my artwork. When lockdown started, I decided it was finally the time to build my own doll-house in which I would indulge myself by having a gallery and cafe.

I have a life-size scale gallery in Spain (www.pocagallery.com) where, partly because of lockdown and distance, I cannot be as involved as I would like.

This was my first ever build so it is a bit rough on the edges, but it was a much-needed substitute for not being able to see art in person and also for building something with my hands as opposed to all these virtual/online exhibitions.

It was also a chance to build a home for my own collection of little works by others. It got such a great response on Instagram that I decided to exhibit other artists work in it as well.

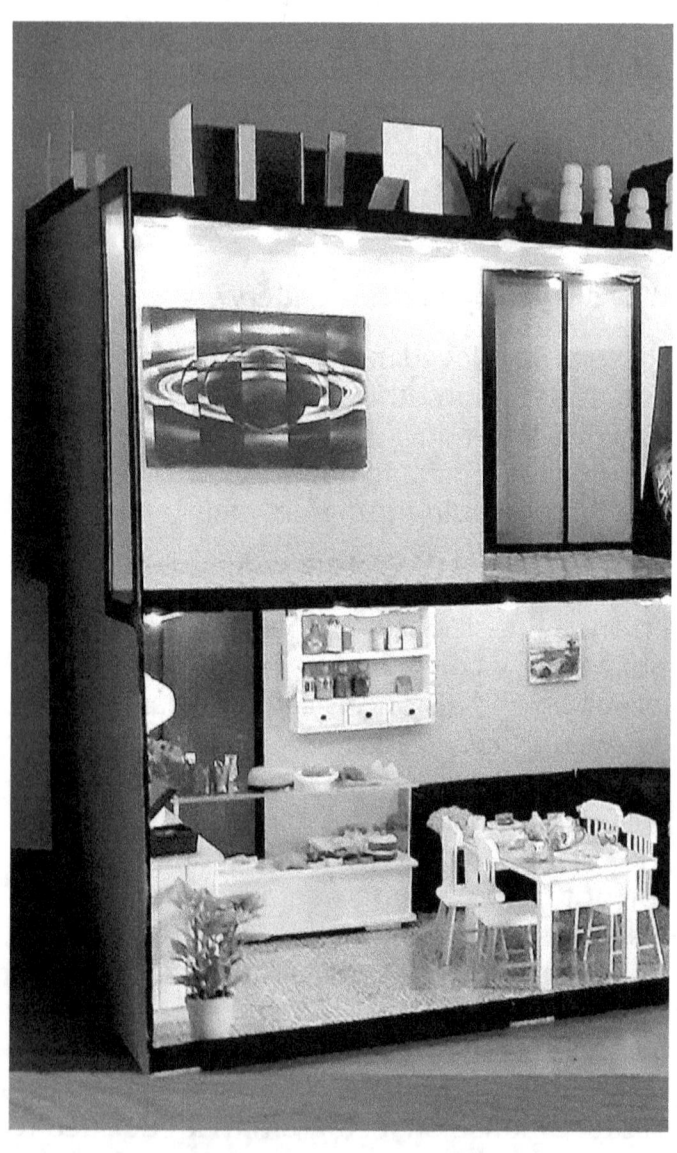

Beyond Scale gallery interior showing cafe and gallery space above.

What do you exhibit?

I am interested in exhibiting contemporary work that is not a replica of another existing work, that is small by nature or experiments and plays with scale.

I want artists to make the most of the intimate immensity afforded by miniature.

There are no submissions guidelines or deadlines and I am open to ideas from any artist!

What do you wish you had known before you opened your gallery?

I guess some practical things about building a model, like lighting and the importance of ceiling height!

But I learned a lot as I went along simply by trial and error so I am already planning some building work on the gallery or possibly a full rebuild!

What is the best thing about running a tiny gallery?

It has all the best things that any miniature offers, a sense of control and freedom of imagination, a bit of escapism I guess.

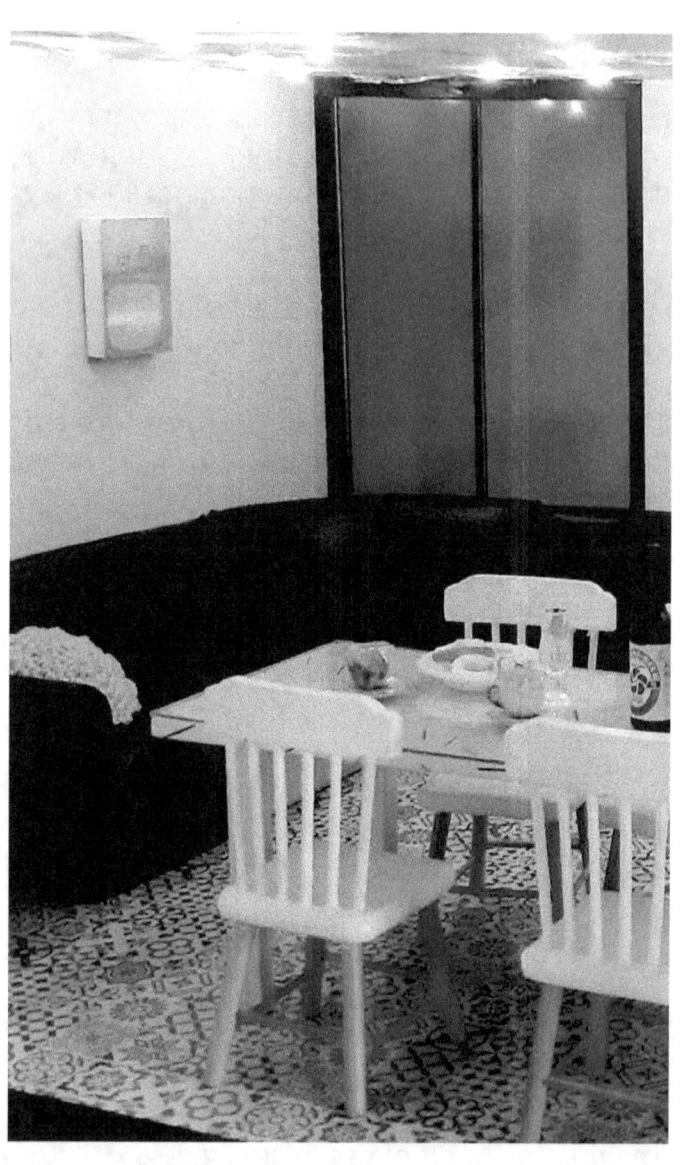
The cafe at Beyond Space Gallery.

Miniatures, especially during this time of virtual/screen-based increased presence, enable a sort of remote yet close encounter, they occupy a physical real space — they have a haptic quality — while also being an object to be consumed mainly through vision.

All this also has the downside of course that most people will only access my gallery through Instagram or the blog at the moment, but I hope that after lockdown I will be able to have the gallery somewhere for people to enjoy it in person.

It, I hope, also enables the artists (certainly it has done to me) to think big with their work and experiment with scales in a much more affordable way. It is also so easy to install and take down a show (haha!).

What advice would you give someone starting a tiny gallery?

Just go for it! Don't think too much, just buy some cheap materials and start trying. Do it first of all for yourself.

My practical advice would be to make the ceilings higher than you think and to incorporate lighting as part of the build if you can!

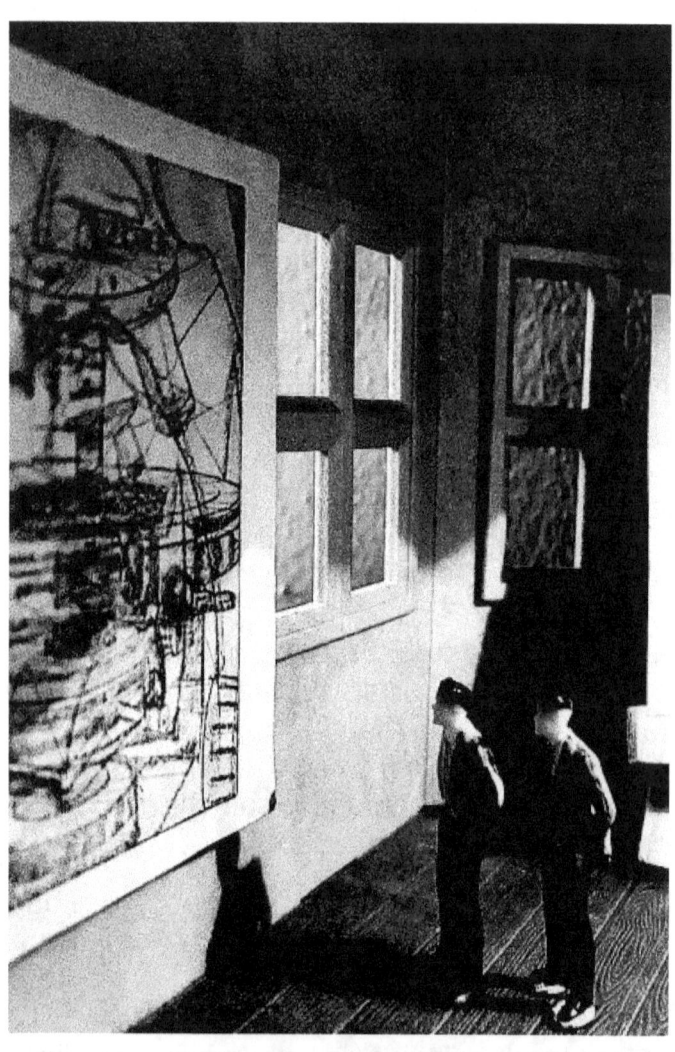

Small scale replica of the print 'Microscope Framework' from the series' reimagining reality' by Anna Marris at the Struwig Miniature Gallery (Room 3).

Struwig Miniature Gallery

Gallery inside a dolls house.
Instagram: @tiffany_struwig_fine_art

Why did you open a tiny gallery?

I opened a tiny gallery primarily as a response to the pandemic. Going into lockdown meant the whole creative community was hit hard.

Fine art was no exception. Galleries shut, exhibitions were cancelled, and studio spaces were abandoned. Those that had large scale work were no longer able to show or even access what they had made and even those that worked small were left adrift.

So, everything moved online, and we all began working small. We found what would work in times where we didn't always have a luxury of space. Desks became easels, walls became exhibitions and video calls became private views.

The art community would not be crushed. If we are good at anything its being creative in the face of adversity.

I had already begun to include aspects of scale manipulation and set building within my practice and it seemed like a natural transition for me

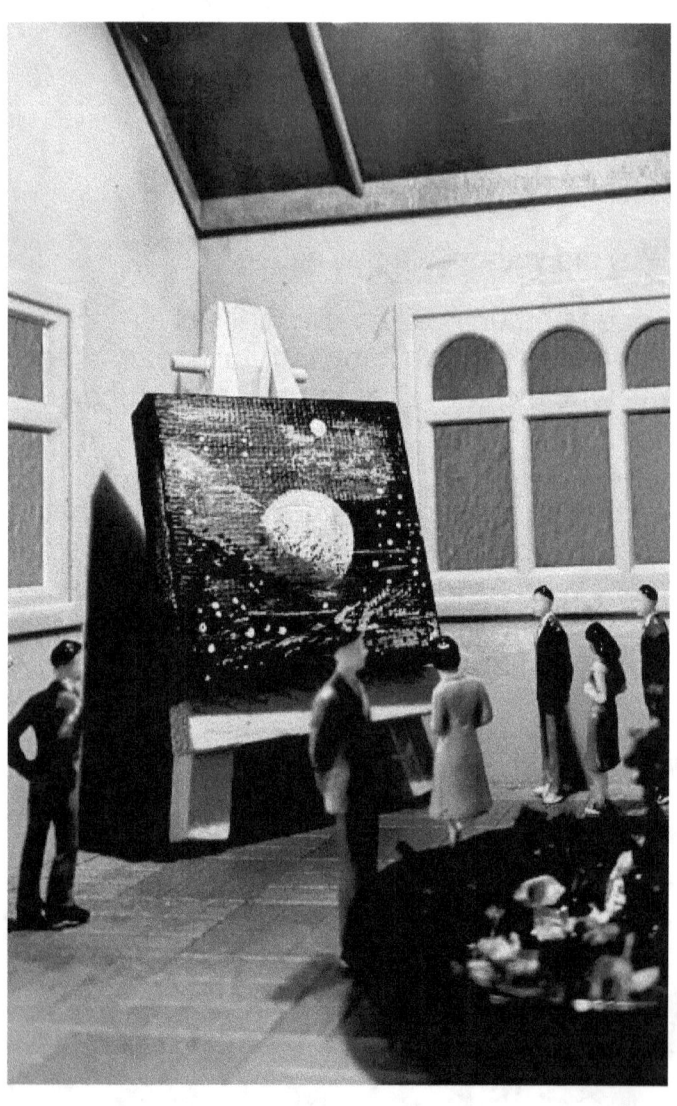

'The Polluted pond' sculpture by Tamzin Wilson and painting 'Not so Distant Body' by Jacob John Hall at Struwig Miniature Gallery (Room2).

to start not only to create my own small scale work, but to begin to curate all the wonderful work my peers were developing unbeknownst to the rest of the world.

What isn't always apparent is that there are far more artists than the world realises. We aren't all in studios readying for exhibitions. There are those that do art part-time, in any spare second they have. They could be your postman, the person scanning your vegetables at the supermarket or that student holding down a minimum wage retail job. Their work is valid, and it deserves to be seen.

What do you exhibit?

I accept any art that fits within the dimensions of the doll-house though my exhibits usually contain small scale prints, paintings and sculpture. Some of the work is created for the purpose of being miniature art and others are small replicas of the large scale work the artist already produces (like Duchamp's suitcase works).

Occasionally there are anomalies, little gateways that allow art to be delivered (and the odd figure to escape). Every time a new piece arrives, they celebrate by hosting private views to contemplate what has been made.

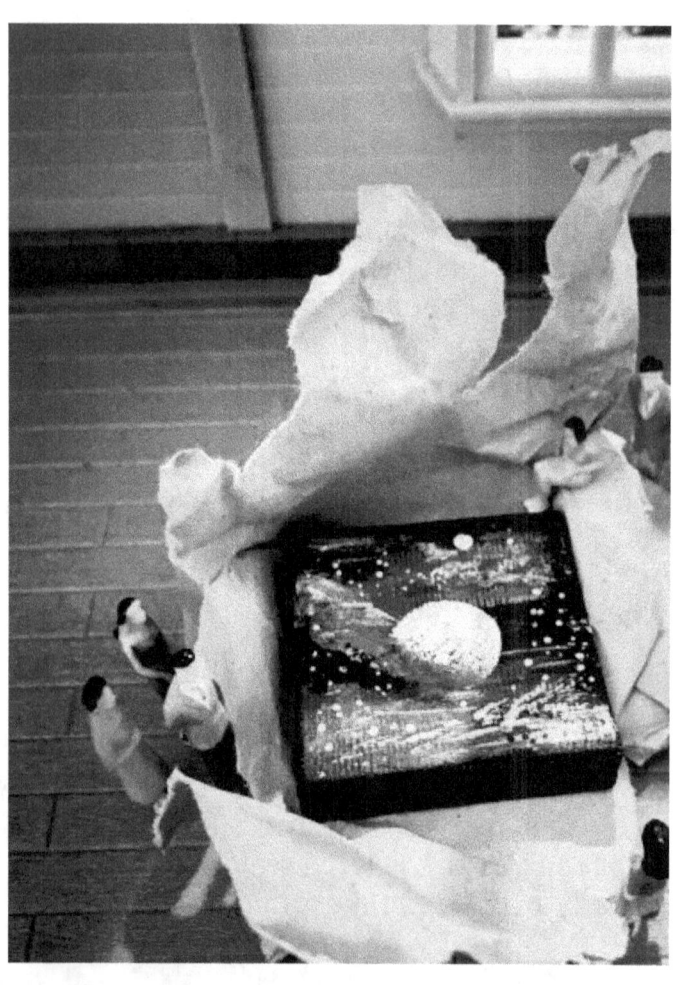

"The narrative of the gallery is that it exists in a world populated by small plastic people who thrive on the art we are able to 'send' to them."

Tiffany Struwig, Struwig Minature Gallery

The photographs are taken in the style of surveillance footage/photography of these events.

What do you wish you had known before you opened your gallery?

A gallery is hard work no matter its scale. Even if the walls are 11 cm tall it must still be curated with as much care as a life size gallery.

Even if it's 1 inch tall, an oil painting the process of drying must be transported with as much reverence as a masterpiece (especially if using public transport).

What is the best thing about running a tiny gallery?

The best thing about running a tiny gallery is seeing how happy the artists are. They are overjoyed at seeing their little works as huge installations, seeing how their work is cherished and admired not despite its scale but because of it.

Nothing brings me more joy than seeing the comments people leave on each post admiring works they may have never gotten to see.

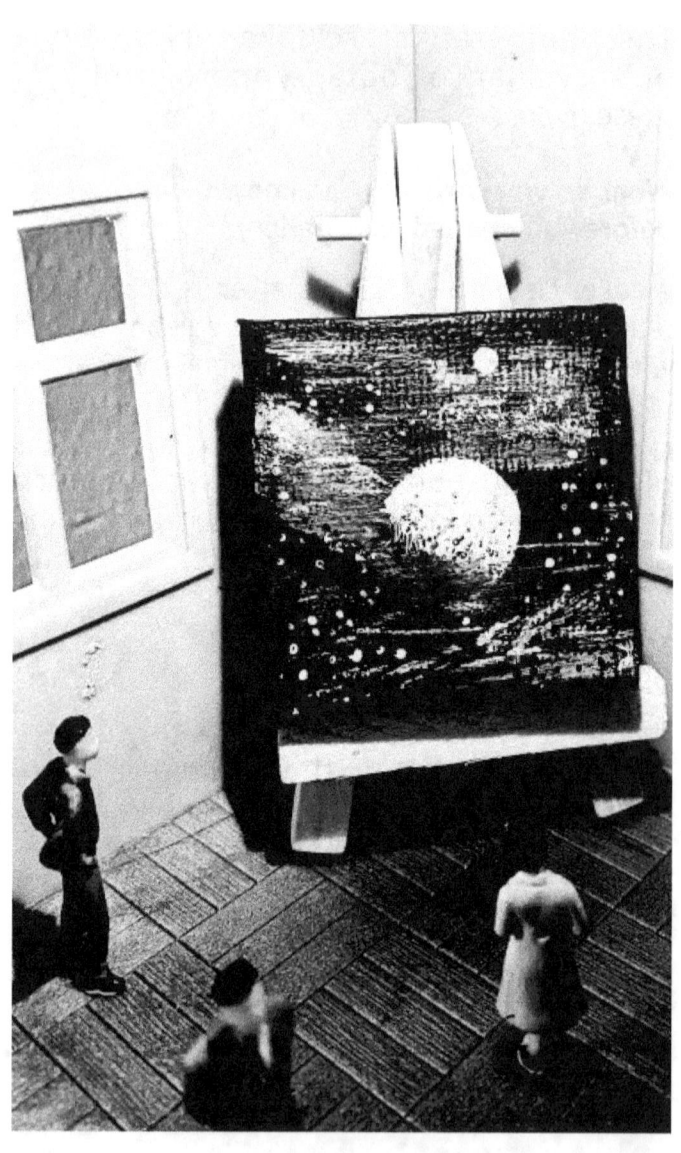

'Not So Distant Body' Painting by Jacob John Hall at the Struwig Miniature Gallery (Room2).

What advice would you give someone starting a tiny gallery?

Even if the exhibition space is small and you believe you have it all planned out think again, roll with the punches and adapt.

Things will go wrong, some pieces work better next to others and your artists will change their minds. Be patient and set achievable goals and deadlines. Be flexible and enjoy yourself.

Anything else you want to mention

Keep making no matter what. This world needs you. Art is vital. No matter how small your work, it can always have a big effect.

"**I am trying to create a space in which artists from all walks of life can have a space to exhibit their work. To see their efforts come to fruition and have their work be seen by the public and the figures populating my gallery.**"

Tiffany Struwig, Struwig Miniature Gallery

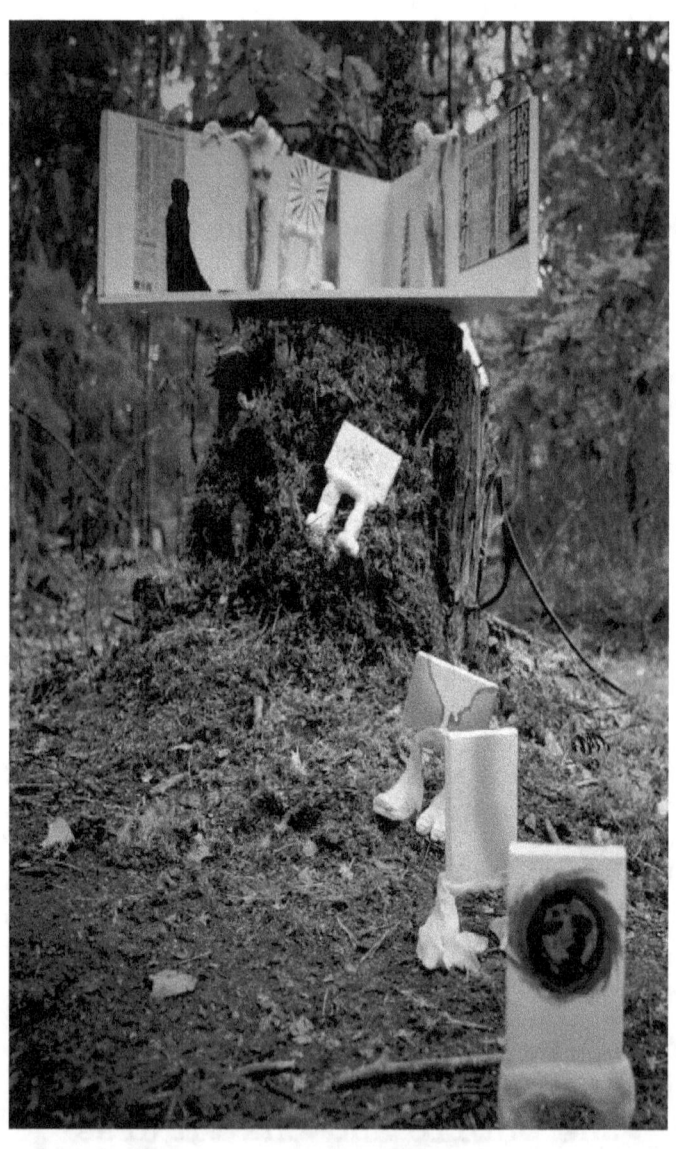

Painting is Also a Human Being. Mini Gallery Don't Cry at Yaga Gathering.

Mini Gallery Don't Cry

Mini Gallery Don't Cry is always open for collaborations or individual projects. They can be off topic, or long-term, questionable, weird — please write to me, let's solve it.

Instagram: @minigallery_dontcry

Why did you open a tiny gallery?

When I really think about 'why?' I guess it is a mixture of how I do like to spend time in between chilling and working. I like to solve things out, rethink different scenarios, play board games, collect things I can't take (shape of trees, holes in architecture, etc.).

My mind is more of a D.I.Y. human and artist, and I paint oil paintings and it is a professional challenge to paint a real tiny oil on canvas. So it just all came together.

I felt bored and tired from normal exhibitions. Wanted to do something about it. Something cool, meaningful and fun. At that point of life I understood that I needed to have a gallery, I must own one, to fulfil some of the beyond normal serving of art. Tiny? Yeah, I can do tiny!

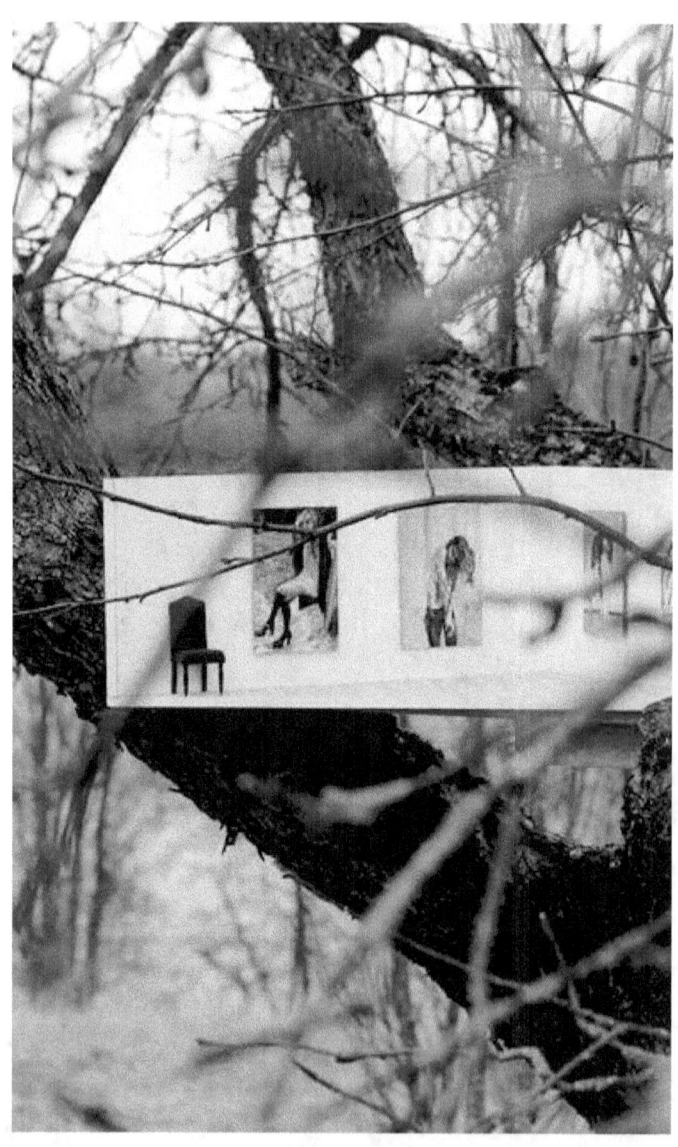

'Escape Plan Failed Let's Stick to Reality' by Kristina Kurilionok at Mini Gallery Don't Cry.

What do you exhibit?

Reviewing all the past exhibitions, seems that paintings are the most exhibited media since my gallery opened in 2014.

It is a challenge to paint a tiny painting and look at it seriously, understanding the reasons and the consequences.

Everything matters — the chosen location for the mood, scenario, the art itself, the vibe altogether, the responsibility for what you show.

What do you wish you had known before you opened your gallery?

I wish I had known more artists who were brave to let the inner child cooperate and conquer what other people think about what is real. Everything that you believe is real.

What is the best thing about running a tiny gallery?

The best thing is that everyone is happy about it. It's magic. People really like small, cute things, we say awwwwwwwww :) It's the same with the tiny gallery — people say awwwwwwwwww :) And it is double best when someone believes in it too. OK, even triple best, when artists take the initiative to participate.

"**To have the opportunity to exhibit inside a cardboard box, allowed me to rethink and scale down my work so it can be seen from a different perspective"**

Sally Eldars, Artist and Curator

Resources

Resources

Books and films

Here are a few literary and cinematic references to scale. Some books have been adapted for cinema many times and it is interesting to see how different directors have worked with the concepts.

Gulliver's Travels

Jonathan Swift 1726.
Gulliver is a surgeon who is shipwrecked on an island populated by tiny people. Film versions include a Technicolor animation from 1939, a 1977 movie that used both live footage and animation and a more recent 2010 film.

The Borrowers

Mary Norton 1952.
Borrowers are tiny people who live under the floorboards and 'borrow' useful items from human 'beans'. They are innovative and inventive, finding new uses for things that they steal from the humans. The BBC produced the Borrowers in 1992 and 2011 and Studio Ghibli animated Arrietty in 2010. Arrietty is the name of the main tiny character.

Alice's Adventures in Wonderland

Lewis Carroll 1865.
Alice falls down a rabbit hole and finds herself in a hallway with many doors. One is too small for her to fit through even though she has a key to open it. She shrinks and grows when she eats and drinks from a bottle labelled 'Drink Me' and a cake labelled 'Eat Me', eventually getting to the right size to fit through the small door. There are loads of versions of Alice in film and on TV. The first is a short silent film from 1903. The artiest is by Jan Švankmajer in 1988 (Alice) and there are many operas, ballets, animations and TV versions.

The Miniaturist

Jessie Burton 2014.
Adapted for TV by the BBC in 2017. It is a beautifully shot mini series that features a dolls house for adults. It is set in Amsterdam in 1686-87 and inspired by Petronella Oortman's doll's house which is on display at the Rijksmuseum. This series gives us some idea of how beautifully decorated the interior of such a hobby dolls house would have been.

Admin

Things to make the administration side of running a gallery easier.

If you are in the UK you will need to be GDPR compliant which basically means that any information you store about people should be stored safely and if requested, you must delete it. This means that if you are keeping a mailing list you must ensure it is safe and can be retrieved at a moments notice. This is something to bear in mind when you keep records.

Google Docs/Sheets

You need a gmail address to access Google Drive which includes the word processing Docs and the spreadsheet Sheets. All the information is stored in the cloud but you can set individual files so that you can work on them offline. Docs and Sheets are good for collaborations because more than one person can work on a file at once.

Airtable

Fantastic resource with many free templates for keeping track of exhibitions and sales. Airtable is a powerful database with multiple applications. The paid for version is more versatile but the free version is brilliant.

Scheduling

Scheduling social media posts can save you hours of work as you can cram a whole weeks worth of posts into a couple of hours. This method also allows you to upload to Instagram from your computer.

Later

Currently allows you to schedule 30 posts to one platform per month for free. Platforms included are Instagram, Twitter, Facebook and Pinterest. The free version allows you to save content which means you can cut and paste hashtags. The paid for version lets you schedule stories, suggests hashtags and the best time to post.

Tailwind

Similar to Later with no free options but unlimited scheduling and a hashtag suggester that shows you if a tag is popular or niche. Tailwind has recently introduced a photo editor. Both Tailwind and later can be used on desktops and mobiles.

Graphic design

An easily identifiable brand makes your gallery look more professional and builds trust among your viewers. There are lots of free resources online that can help you make a logo and posters.

Canva

Easy to use graphic design app. The free version on phone and desktop lets you import images and place text over them. There are loads of templates and pre loaded graphics to help you.

Pixlr

Easy to use photo editing app that helps you edit your images and optimise them for use on a website.

Gimp

Open source programme that is an alternative to Photoshop and wonderful for image manipulation. Gimp is not terribly intuitive to use but is very powerful in the right hands.

Scribus

Open source desk top publishing software which replaces Publisher and InDesign. Perfect for layout if you wanted to make a print version of a catalogue.

Inkscape

Open source alternative to Illustrator for vector graphics.

Hashtag ideas

#artgallery
#smallgallery
#tinygallery
#microgallery
#boxgallery
#artinabox
#smallmodernart
#artexhibition
#artlovers
#artworks
#small
#tiny
#contemporaryart
#modernart
#artcollector
#artshow
#abstractart
#contemporarypainting
#abstractpainting
#gallerist
#gallery
#photography
#visualart

Props and scaled figures

Thingiverse

An online resource that has many free files you can 3D print. There are frames, easels and tiny people which you can scale to your own requirements. It is possible to get 3D printing done remotely, you send an agency a file and they send you back the finished prints. Search for '3D Printing Service' to find one.

Scaled models

For very accurate scaled models look at model railway suppliers. OO scale people are around 2 to 2.5cm tall and you can often buy job lots of them, already painted. There are many other sizes available. Most of the railway people are dressed for outdoors, as they are for placing on platforms.

For a more indoorsy feel, Architectural Scale Figures come in a variety of poses though they are most often unpainted and white. 1:50 scale is around 3.5cm tall.

Search for 'Architectural cut out PNG people' or 'People cut-outs' if you want images of people on a clear background. Search for people silhouettes if you want to cut them out yourself.

Model animals are easy to find in toy shops and it is usually common to find mixed bags of small toy characters in charity shops.

Doll's house suppliers are good for accurate copies of tiny chairs, rugs, wallpaper, windows, stairs and doors.

There is no right way

This book has given you some ideas for ways to make your own tiny gallery. None of these are the right way, none are the wrong way. Tiny Galleries are a law unto themselves and the only rule is to enjoy your time making and curating them.

Think small

Think inside the box

"Tiny galleries don't have to be square they just need that sense of fun."
Jack Woodward, C.B.M Gallery

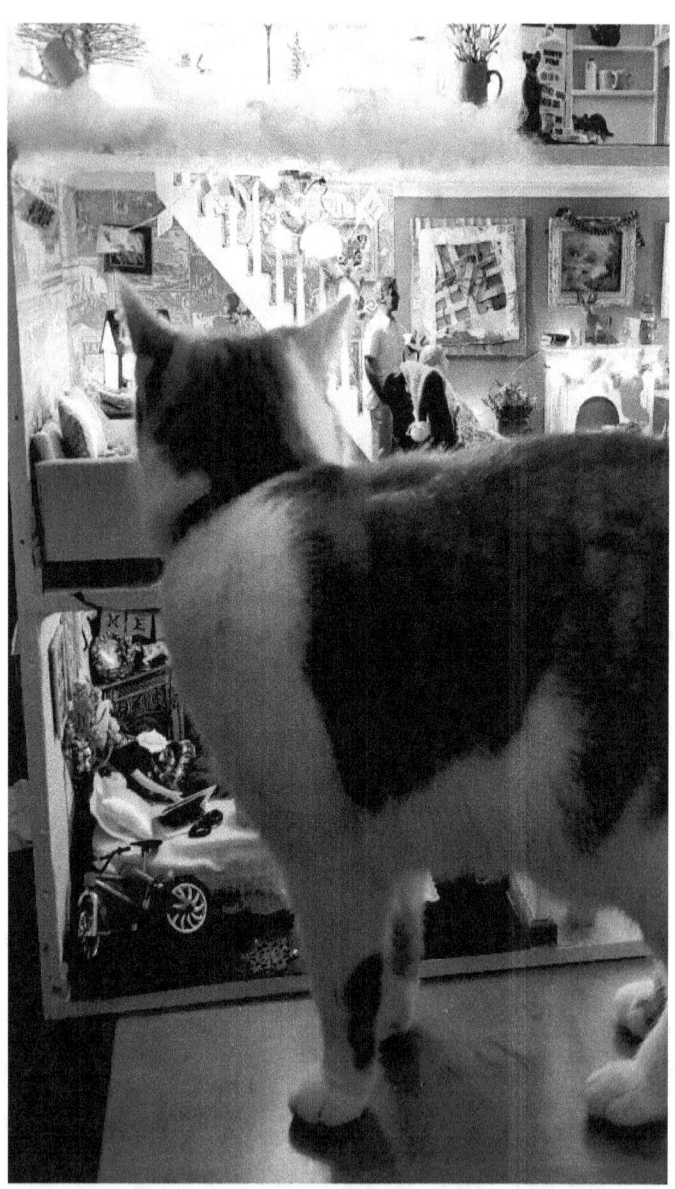

Fudge, in his capacity as building inspector checks all is to his satisfaction at the Doll's House Art Gallery.

www.ingramcontent.com/pod-product-compliance
Lightning Source LLC
Chambersburg PA
CBHW070417220526
45466CB00004B/1438